Carbon Dioxide and Climate:
A Second Assessment

Report of the CO_2/Climate Review Panel
to the
Climate Research Committee of the
Climate Board/Committee on Atmospheric Sciences
and the
Carbon Dioxide Assessment Committee of the
Climate Board

Commission on Physical Sciences, Mathematics, and Resources

National Research Council

NATIONAL ACADEMY PRESS
Washington, D.C.   1982

NOTICE The project that is the subject of this report was approved by the Governing Board of the National Research Council, whose members are drawn from the councils of the National Academy of Sciences, the National Academy of Engineering, and the Institute of Medicine. The members of the committee responsible for the report were chosen for their special competences and with regard for appropriate balance.

This report has been reviewed by a group other than the authors according to procedures approved by a Report Review Committee consisting of members of the National Academy of Sciences, the National Academy of Engineering, and the Institute of Medicine.

The National Research Council was established by the National Academy of Sciences in 1916 to associate the broad community of science and technology with the Academy's purposes of furthering knowledge and of advising the federal government. The Council operates in accordance with general policies determined by the Academy under the authority of its congressional charter of 1863, which establishes the Academy as a private, nonprofit, self-governing membership corporation. The Council has become the principal operating agency of both the National Academy of Sciences and the National Academy of Engineering in the conduct of their services to the government, the public, and the scientific and engineering communities. It is administered jointly by both Academies and the Institute of Medicine. The National Academy of Engineering and the Institute of Medicine were established in 1964 and 1970, respectively, under the charter of the National Academy of Sciences.

Library of Congress Cataloging in Publication Data

National Research Council (U.S.). CO_2/Climate
  Review Panel.
  Carbon dioxide and climate.

  Bibliography: p.
  1. Atmospheric carbon dioxide—Research—United States. 2. United States—Climate. I. National Research Council (U.S.). Climate Research Committee. II. National Research Council (U.S.). Climate Board. Carbon Dioxide Assessment Committee. III. Title.
  QC879.8.N37   1982   551.6   82-12445
  ISBN 0-309-03285-7

Available from

NATIONAL ACADEMY PRESS
2101 Constitution Avenue, N.W.
Washington, D.C. 20418

Printed in the United States of America

CO_2/Climate Review Panel

Joseph Smagorinsky, Geophysical Fluid Dynamics Laboratory, National Oceanic and Atmospheric Administration, *Chairman*
Laurence Armi, Scripps Institution of Oceanography
Francis P. Bretherton, National Center for Atmospheric Research
Kirk Bryan, Geophysical Fluid Dynamics Laboratory, National Oceanic and Atmospheric Administration
Robert D. Cess, State University of New York, Stony Brook
W. Lawrence Gates, Oregon State University
James Hansen, Goddard Institute for Space Studies, National Aeronautics and Space Administration
John E. Kutzbach, University of Wisconsin, Madison
Syukuro Manabe, Geophysical Fluid Dynamics Laboratory, National Oceanic and Atmospheric Administration

Invited Experts

William W. Kellogg, National Center for Atmospheric Research
V. Ramanathan, National Center for Atmospheric Research
Stephen H. Schneider, National Center for Atmospheric Research

Staff

John S. Perry, National Research Council, *Executive Secretary*
Robert S. Chen, National Academy of Sciences, *Resident Fellow*

Climate Research Committee

Joseph Smagorinsky, Geophysical Fluid Dynamics Laboratory, National Oceanic and Atmospheric Administration, *Chairman*
D. James Baker, Jr., University of Washington
Tim P. Barnett, Scripps Institution of Oceanography
Harry L. Bryden, Woods Hole Oceanographic Institution
W. Lawrence Gates, Oregon State University
John E. Kutzbach, University of Wisconsin, Madison
Syukuro Manabe, Geophysical Fluid Dynamics Laboratory, National Oceanic and Atmospheric Administration
Allan R. Robinson, Harvard University
Thomas H. Vonder Haar, Colorado State University
John M. Wallace, University of Washington
Gunter E. Weller, University of Alaska

Carbon Dioxide Assessment Committee

William A. Nierenberg, Scripps Institution of Oceanography, *Chairman*
Peter G. Brewer, National Science Foundation
Lester Machta, Air Resources Laboratory, National Oceanic and Atmospheric Administration
William D. Nordhaus, Yale University
Roger R. Revelle, University of California, San Diego
Thomas C. Schelling, Harvard University
Joseph Smagorinsky, Geophysical Fluid Dynamics Laboratory, National Oceanic and Atmospheric Administration
Paul E. Waggoner, Connecticut Agricultural Experiment Station
George M. Woodwell, Marine Biological Laboratory

Committee on Atmospheric Sciences

Richard J. Reed, University of Washington, *Chairman*
Verner E. Suomi, University of Wisconsin, Madison, *Vice Chairman*
David Atlas, National Aeronautics and Space Administration
Ferdinand Baer, University of Maryland
Ralph J. Cicerone, National Center for Atmospheric Research
Robert E. Dickinson, National Center for Atmospheric Research
John A. Dutton, Pennsylvania State University
John V. Evans, Massachusetts Institute of Technology
Peter V. Hobbs, University of Washington
T. N. Krishnamurti, Florida State University
James C. McWilliams, National Center for Atmospheric Research
F. Sherwood Rowland, University of California, Irvine
Frederick Sanders, Massachusetts Institute of Technology
Friedrich Schott, University of Miami

Liaison with Federal Agencies

Richard S. Greenfield, National Science Foundation
Ronald L. Lavoie, National Oceanic and Atmospheric Administration

Staff

Fred D. White, *Executive Secretary*

Climate Board

Verner E. Suomi, University of Wisconsin, Madison, *Chairman*
Philip Abelson, American Association for the Advancement of Science
William C. Ackermann, University of Illinois at Urbana-Champaign
Werner A. Baum, Florida State University
Francis P. Bretherton, National Center for Atmospheric Research
Dayton H. Clewell, Darien, Connecticut
Thomas M. Donahue, University of Michigan
Joseph O. Fletcher, National Oceanic and Atmospheric Administration
Robert W. Kates, Clark University
John E. Kutzbach, University of Wisconsin, Madison
Estella B. Leopold, University of Washington
William A. Nierenberg, Scripps Institution of Oceanography
Roger R. Revelle, University of California, San Diego
Joseph Smagorinsky, National Oceanic and Atmospheric Administration
Sylvan H. Wittwer, Michigan State University
Warren S. Wooster, University of Washington

Staff

John S. Perry, National Research Council, *Executive Secretary*
Robert S. Chen, National Academy of Sciences, *Resident Fellow*

Liaison with Federal Agencies

Eugene W. Bierly, National Science Foundation
Alan D. Hecht, National Climate Program Office
Norman L. Canfield, National Oceanic and Atmospheric Administration
Galen Hart, Department of Agriculture
Gerald J. Kovach, Committee on Commerce, Science and Transportation, U.S. Senate
David W. McClintock, Department of State
Lloyd J. Money, Department of Transportation
Robert E. Palmer, U.S. House of Representatives
George I. Smith, Department of the Interior
Joel A. Snow, Department of Energy
Shelby G. Tilford, National Aeronautics and Space Administration
Paul D. Try, Department of Defense
Herbert L. Wiser, Environmental Protection Agency

Commission on Physical Sciences, Mathematics, and Resources

Herbert Friedman, National Research Council, *Cochairman*
Robert M. White, University Corporation for Atmospheric Research, *Cochairman*
Stanley I. Auerbach, Oak Ridge National Laboratory
Elkan R. Blout, Harvard Medical School
William Browder, Princeton University
Bernard F. Burke, Massachusetts Institute of Technology
Herman Chernoff, Massachusetts Institute of Technology
Walter R. Eckelmann, Exxon Corporation
Joseph L. Fisher, Office of the Governor, Commonwealth of Virginia
James C. Fletcher, University of Pittsburgh
William A. Fowler, California Institute of Technology
Gerhart Friedlander, Brookhaven National Laboratory
Edward A. Frieman, Science Applications, Inc.
Edward D. Goldberg, Scripps Institution of Oceanography
Konrad B. Krauskopf, Stanford University
Charles J. Mankin, Oklahoma Geological Survey
Walter H. Munk, University of California, San Diego
Norton Nelson, New York University Medical Center
Daniel A. Okun, University of North Carolina
George E. Pake, Xerox Research Center
David Pimentel, Cornell University
Charles K. Reed, National Research Council
Hatten S. Yoder, Jr., Carnegie Institution of Washington

Raphael G. Kasper, *Acting Executive Director*

Foreword

As residents of this most pleasant planet, we must necessarily be concerned about any changes in its heating and ventilation systems. One possibly significant change has been unequivocally observed over the past two decades: the amount of carbon dioxide in the air has increased. Moreover, it seems almost certain that we are primarily to blame. By burning fossil fuels and converting the carbon-rich natural landscape into farmland and cities, we transfer carbon to the atmosphere. Since carbon dioxide absorbs and emits thermal radiation and is an essential nutrient for plants, there is good reason to suspect that increases in its abundance may affect the climate of the globe and the workings of the biological systems that support our life.

As we plan ways of meeting our energy needs from fossil fuel and alternative sources, it is thus prudent to consider the implications for atmospheric carbon dioxide, climate, agriculture, the natural biosphere, and indeed for our increasingly interdependent global society. In framing the Energy Security Act of 1980, the Congress requested the Office of Science and Technology Policy and the National Academy of Sciences to conduct a comprehensive assessment of the implications of increasing carbon dioxide due to fossil fuel use and other human activities. The Climate Board of the National Research Council was asked to assume responsibility for the study, and the Carbon Dioxide Assessment Committee was formed under the board's aegis. Our assessment will deal with many questions relating to this complex issue: What amounts of fossil fuel are likely to be burned? How much carbon dioxide may remain in the air? What may be the effects on agriculture? How may these changes interact with other changes in a rapidly evolving world?

At this writing, work is under way on these and other elements that will be integrated into our report.

It was evident, however, that one aspect of the carbon dioxide issue merited early attention. The influence of higher levels of atmospheric carbon dioxide on climate was assessed in 1979 by a panel chaired by the late Jule G. Charney. Since then, much work has been done, and some questions have been raised. An updated assessment of the relationship between carbon dioxide and climate was clearly in order, and Joseph Smagorinsky, Director of the Geophysical Fluid Dynamics Laboratory of the National Oceanic and Atmospheric Administration, was requested to lead a panel to address this task. This is the panel's report. It will contribute to the assessment to be prepared by the Carbon Dioxide Assessment Committee, but it also stands in its own right as a significant addition to our understanding of this complex and worrisome issue. I believe that it should also serve as a continuing reminder of the genius and wisdom of Jule G. Charney, who illuminated this question as he did so many other problems of science and mankind.

William A. Nierenberg, *Chairman*
Carbon Dioxide Assessment Committee

Preface

In the summer of 1979, the Director of the Office of Science and Technology Policy (OSTP) requested the President of the National Academy of Sciences to conduct a special study to assess the then current state of knowledge regarding the possible effects of increased atmospheric carbon dioxide (CO_2) on climate. A committee under the chairmanship of the late Jule G. Charney was formed and produced a report (Climate Research Board, 1979), hereafter referred to as the Charney report.

In the intervening years, the National Research Council (NRC) formed the Carbon Dioxide Assessment Committee under its Climate Board (formerly the Climate Research Board). The committee's responsibility to the OSTP, at the request of the Congress, is to provide an overview of the entire CO_2 question. In this pursuit, the Carbon Dioxide Assessment Committee has asked the Climate Research Committee of the Climate Board (CB) and the Committee on Atmospheric Sciences (CAS) to bring up to date the Charney report, while essentially retaining the focus confined to the CO_2–climate connection. The timeliness of such an update stems from the accelerated research activity on the many facets of the problem stimulated by vigorous national and international public attention. The subjects covered in the present report, therefore, generally coincide with those in the 1979 report, but some new considerations have been included, reflecting a broadened base of understanding of the problem. Examples are the role of aerosols, the development of climate scenarios, and some issues relating to development of a monitoring strategy for early detection.

The present *ad hoc* CO_2/Climate Review Panel, including invited experts, was established by the joint CB/CAS Climate Research Committee. Three meetings of the panel were held in March, April, and July 1981. The last of these took place at the National Center for Atmospheric Research, and we appreciate greatly the center's hospitality and the opportunity for discussions with its expert research staff. Staff support for the panel's work was provided by Robert S. Chen and John S. Perry of the CB staff, and Doris Bouadjemi and Sally Larisch speedily processed innumerable corrections and interim drafts. The panel is most grateful for the contributions of the invited experts who assisted in its work and are cited in the list of its members. In particular, V. Ramanathan and Stephen H. Schneider made major contributions to the discussion of energy-balance models. The panel's draft report was reviewed by members of the original Charney panel, other experts, the panel's parent committees, and the NRC's Report Review Committee.

The report discusses at length two recent studies that have concluded that the effect of increased CO_2 on surface temperatures will be much less than estimated by the majority of the scientific community. The panel believes that these studies are flawed and incomplete, and the report attempts to identify clearly their deficiencies. The authors of the dissenting studies were provided with an opportunity to review the panel's report but remain unconvinced. Ultimately, of course, nature will reveal to us all the truth.

The panel believes that, with the rapid rate of development of some of the scientific foundations on which firmer conclusions can be drawn, the problem will warrant periodic reassessments.

Joseph Smagorinsky, *Chairman*
CO_2/Climate Review Panel

Contents

SUMMARY OF CONCLUSIONS AND RECOMMENDATIONS   1

1 INTRODUCTION AND OVERVIEW   9

2 PRINCIPAL SCIENTIFIC ISSUES IN MODELING STUDIES   15

Global Climate Sensitivity—Simplified Models and Empirical Approaches, 15
One-dimensional models, 15
Surface energy balance considerations, 17
Models of the Earth's complete energy balance, 17
Dissenting inferences from energy-balance models and empirical studies, 18

Role of the Oceans, 24
Role of the ocean in the transient response of climate, 24
Effects of sea ice, 30

Cloud Effects, 31
Cloudiness–radiation feedback, 31
Stratus–sea-ice interactions, 33

Trace Gases Other Than CO_2, 34

Atmospheric Aerosols, 37

Validation of Climate Models, 39
Need for model validation, 39
Present state of model validation, 40

Planetary studies, 43
Alternative modeling approaches, 45
Improvement of model validation, 46

3 PREDICTIONS AND SCENARIOS OF CLIMATE CHANGES DUE TO CO_2 INCREASES   48

Development of Predictions and Scenarios, 48

Model Studies, 50
Numerical experiments with climate models, 50
Global-average response, 50
Zonal-average response, 53
Geographical distribution of climate changes, 55

Observational Studies of Contemporary and Past Climates, 56
Use of observational studies, 56
Contemporary climatic data, 56
Past climatic data, 58

4 DEVELOPMENT OF MONITORING AND EARLY DETECTION STRATEGIES   61

Current Status, 61
Detection Strategies, 61
Monitoring Ocean Climate Response, 63

REFERENCES   65

Summary of Conclusions and Recommendations

For over a century, concern has been expressed that increases in atmospheric carbon dioxide (CO_2) concentration could affect global climate by changing the heat balance of the atmosphere and Earth. Observations reveal steadily increasing concentrations of CO_2, and experiments with numerical climate models indicate that continued increase would eventually produce significant climatic change. Comprehensive assessment of the issue will require projection of future CO_2 emissions and study of the disposition of this excess carbon in the atmosphere, ocean, and biota; the effect on climate; and the implications for human welfare. This study focuses on one aspect, estimation of the effect on climate of assumed future increases in atmospheric CO_2. Conclusions are drawn principally from present-day numerical models of the climate system. To address the significant role of the oceans, the study also makes use of observations of the distributions of anthropogenic tracers other than CO_2. The rapid scientific developments in these areas suggest that periodic reassessments will be warranted.

The starting point for the study was a similar 1979 review by a Climate Research Board panel chaired by the late Jule G. Charney. *The present study has not found any new results that necessitate substantial revision of the conclusions of the Charney report.*

SIMPLIFIED CLIMATE MODELS AND EMPIRICAL STUDIES

Numerical models of the climate system are the primary tools for investigating human impact on climate. Simplified models permit economically feasible analyses over a wide range of conditions. Although they can provide only limited information on local or regional effects, simplified models are valuable for focusing and interpreting studies performed with more complete and realistic models. *The sensitivity of global-mean temperature to increased atmospheric CO_2 estimated from simplified models is generally consistent with that estimated from more complete models.*

The effects of increased CO_2 are usually stated in terms of surface temperature, and models of the energy balance at the surface are often employed for their estimation. However, changes in atmospheric CO_2 actually affect the energy balance of the entire climate system. *Because of the strong coupling between the surface and the atmosphere, global-mean surface warming is driven by radiative heating of the entire surface–atmosphere system, not only by the direct radiative heating at the surface.*

Theoretical and empirical studies of the climatic effects of increased CO_2 must properly account for all significant processes involved, notably changes in the tropospheric energy budget and the effects of ocean storage and atmospheric and oceanic transport of heat. For example, studies of the isolated surface energy balance or local observational studies of the transient response to short-term radiative changes can result in misleading conclusions. Otherwise, such studies can grossly underestimate or, in some instances, overestimate the long-term equilibrium warming to be expected from increased CO_2. Surface energy balance approaches and empirical studies are fully consistent with comprehensive climate models employed for CO_2 sensitivity studies, provided that the globally connected energy storage and transport processes in the entire climate system are fully accounted for on the appropriate time scales. Indeed, *empirical approaches to estimating climatic sensitivity—particularly those employing satellite radiation budget measurements—should be encouraged.*

ROLE OF THE OCEANS

The heat capacity of the upper ocean is potentially great enough to slow down substantially the response of climate to increasing atmospheric CO_2. The upper ocean will affect both the detection of CO_2-induced climatic changes and the assessment of their likely social implications. The thermal time constant of the atmosphere coupled to the wind-mixed layer of the ocean is only 2–3 years. The thermal time constant of the atmosphere coupled to the upper 500 m of the ocean is roughly 10 times greater, or 20–30 years. On a time scale of a few decades, the deep water below 500 m can act as a sink of heat, slowing the rise of surface temperature. However, tracer data indicate that the globally averaged mixing rate into the deep ocean appears

Summary of Conclusions and Recommendations

to be too slow for it to be of dominant importance on a global scale for time scales less than 100 years.

The lagging ocean thermal response may cause important regional differences in climatic response to increasing CO_2. The response in areas downwind from major oceans will certainly be different from that in the interior of major continents, and a significantly slower response to increasing CO_2 might be expected in the southern hemisphere. *The role of the ocean in time-dependent climatic response deserves special attention in future modeling studies, stressing the regional nature of oceanic thermal inertia and atmospheric energy-transfer mechanisms.*

Progress in understanding the ocean's role must be based on a broad program of research: continued observations of density distributions, tracers, heat fluxes, and ocean currents; quantitative elucidation of the mixing processes potentially involved; substantial theoretical effort; and development of models adequate to reproduce the relative magnitudes of a variety of competing effects. The problems are difficult, and complete success is unlikely to come quickly. Meanwhile, partially substantiated assumptions like those asserted here are likely to remain an integral part of any assessment. In planning the oceanographic field experiments in connection with the World Climate Research Program, *particular attention should be paid to improving estimates of mixing time scales in the main thermocline.*

Present knowledge of the interaction of sea-ice formation and deep-water formation is still rudimentary, and it will be difficult to say even qualitatively what role sea ice will play in high-latitude response and deep-water formation until the climatic factors that control the areal extent of polar pack ice in the northern and southern hemispheres are known. Field experiments are required to gain fundamental observational data concerning these processes.

CLOUD EFFECTS

Cloud amounts, heights, optical properties, and structure may be influenced by CO_2-induced climatic changes. In view of the uncertainties in our knowledge of cloud parameters and the crudeness of cloud-prediction schemes in existing climate models, *it is premature to draw conclusions regarding the influence of clouds on climate sensitivity to increased CO_2.* Empirical approaches, including satellite-observed radiation budget data, are an important means of studying the cloudiness–radiation problem, and they should be pursued.

Simplified climate models indicate that lowering of albedo owing to decreased areal extent of snow and ice contributes substantially to CO_2 warming at high latitudes. However, more complex models suggest that increases in low-level stratus cloud cover may at least partially offset this decrease in albedo. In view of the great oversimplification in the calculation of clouds in climate models, these inferences must be considered tentative.

OTHER TRACE GASES

Although the radiative effects of trace gases (nitrous oxide, methane, ozone, and chlorofluoromethanes) are in most instances additive, their concentrations can be chemically coupled. *The climatic effects of alterations in the concentrations of trace gases can be substantial.*

Since trace-gas abundances might change significantly in the future because of anthropogenic emissions or as a consequence of CO_2-initiated climatic changes, *it is important to monitor the most radiatively significant trace gases.*

ATMOSPHERIC AEROSOLS

Atmospheric aerosols are a potentially significant source of climate variability, but their effects depend on their composition, size, and vertical–global distributions. Stratospheric aerosols consisting mainly of aqueous sulfuric acid droplets, which persist for a few years following major volcanic eruptions, can produce a substantial, but temporary, reduction in global surface temperature and can explain much of the observed natural climatic variability. While stratospheric aerosols may contribute to the infrared greenhouse effect, their net influence appears to be surface cooling.

The climatic effect of tropospheric aerosols—sulfates, marine salts, and wind-blown dust—is much less certain, in part because of inadequate observations and understanding of the optical properties. Although anthropogenic aerosols are particularly noticeable in regions near and downwind of their sources, there does not appear to have been a significant long-term increase in the aerosol level in remote regions of the globe other than possibly the Arctic. *The climatic impact of changes in anthropogenic aerosols, if they occur, cannot currently be determined.* One cannot even conclude that possible future anthropogenic changes in aerosol loading would produce worldwide heating or cooling, although carbon-containing Arctic aerosol definitely causes local atmospheric heating. Increased tropospheric aerosols could also influence cloud optical properties and thus modify cloudiness–radiation feedback. This possibility requires further study.

Summary of Conclusions and Recommendations

THE LAND SURFACE

Land-surface processes also influence climate, and the treatment of surface albedo and evapotranspiration in climate models influences the behavior of climate models. Land-surface processes largely depend on vegetation coverage and may interact with climatic changes in ways that are as yet poorly understood.

VALIDATION OF CLIMATE MODELS

Mathematical-physical models, whether in a highly simplified form or as elaborate formulations of the behavior and interactions of the global atmosphere, ocean, cryosphere, and biomass, are generally considered to be the most powerful tools yet devised for the study of climate. Our confidence in them comes from tests of the correctness of the models' representation of the physical processes and from comparisons of the models' responses to known seasonal variations. Because decisions of immense social and economic importance may be made on the basis of model experiments, *it is important that a comprehensive climate-model validation effort be pursued, including the assembly of a wide variety of observational data specifically for model validation and the development of a validation methodology.*

Validation of climate models involves a hierarchy of tests, including checks on the internal behavior of subsystems of the model. The parameters used in comprehensive climate models are explicitly derived, as much as possible, from comparisons with observations and/or are derived from known physical principles. *Arbitrary adjustment or tuning of climate models is therefore greatly limited.*

The primary method for validating a climate model is to determine how well the model-simulated climate compares with observations. *Comparisons of simulated time means of a number of climatic variables with observations show that modern climate models provide a reasonably satisfactory simulation of the present large-scale global climate and its average seasonal changes.*

More complete validation of models depends on assembly of suitable data, comparison of higher-order statistics, confirmation of the models' representation of physical processes, and verification of ice models.

One test of climate theory can be obtained from empirical examination of other planets that in effect provide an ensemble of experiments over a variety of conditions. *Observed surface temperatures of Mars, Earth, and Venus confirm the existence, nature, and magnitude of the greenhouse effect.*

Laboratory experiments on the behavior of differentially heated rotating fluids have provided insights into the hydrodynamics of the atmosphere and ocean circulations and can contribute to our understanding of processes such as small-scale turbulence and mixing. However, they cannot simulate adequately the most important physical processes involved in climatic change.

Improvement of our confidence in the ability of climate models to assess the climatic impacts of increased CO_2 will require development of model validation methods, including determination of the models' statistical properties; assembly of standardized data for validation; development of observations to validate representations of physical processes; standardization of sensitivity tests; development of physical–dynamical and phenomenological diagnostic techniques focusing on changes specifically attributable to increased CO_2; and use of information from planetary atmospheres, laboratory experiments, and especially contemporary and past climates (see below).

PREDICTIONS AND SCENARIOS

A primary objective of climate-model development is to enable prediction of the response of the climate system to internal or external changes such as increases in atmospheric CO_2. Predictions consist of estimates of the probability of future climatic conditions and unavoidably involve many uncertainties. *Model-derived estimates of globally averaged temperature changes, and perhaps changes averaged along latitude circles, appear to have some predictive reliability for a prescribed CO_2 perturbation.* On the other hand, estimates with greater detail and including other important variables, e.g., windiness, soil moisture, cloudiness, solar insolation, are not yet sufficiently reliable. *Nevertheless, internally consistent and detailed specifications of hypothetical climatic conditions over space and time—"scenarios"—may be quite useful research tools for analysis of social responses and sensitivities to climatic changes.*

INFERENCES FROM CLIMATE MODELS

While present models are not sufficiently realistic to provide reliable predictions in the detail desired for assessment of most impacts, they can still suggest scales and ranges of temporal and spatial variations that can be incorporated into scenarios of possible climatic change.

Mathematical models of climate of a wide range of complexity have been used to estimate changes in the equilibrium climate that would result from an increase in atmospheric CO_2. The main statistically significant conclusions of these studies may be summarized as follows:

1. *The 1979 Charney report estimated the equilibrium global surface warming from a doubling of CO_2 to be "near 3°C with a probable error of*

Summary of Conclusions and Recommendations

$\pm 1.5°C$." No substantial revision of this conclusion is warranted at this time.

2. Both radiative–convective and general-circulation models indicate a cooling of the stratosphere with relatively small latitudinal variation.

3. The global-mean rates of both evaporation and precipitation are projected to increase.

4. Increases in surface air temperature would vary significantly with latitude and over the seasons:

(a) Warming would be 2–3 times as great over the polar regions as over the tropics; warming would be significantly greater over the Arctic than over the Antarctic.

(b) Temperature increases would have large seasonal variations over the Arctic, with minimum warming in summer and maximum warming in winter. In lower latitudes (equatorward of 45° latitude) the warming has smaller seasonal variation.

5. Some qualitative inferences on hydrological changes averaged around latitude circles may be drawn from model simulations:

(a) Annual-mean runoff increases over polar and surrounding regions.

(b) Snowmelt arrives earlier and snowfall begins later.

(c) Summer soil moisture decreases in middle and high latitudes of the northern hemisphere.

(d) The coverage and thickness of sea ice over the Arctic and circum-Antarctic oceans decrease.

Improvement in the quality and resolution of geographical estimates of climatic change will require increased computational resolution in the mathematical models employed, improvement in the representation of the multitude of participating physical processes, better understanding of airflow over and around mountains, and extended time integration of climate models. It is clear, however, that local climate has a much larger temporal variability than climate averaged along latitude circles or over the globe.

OBSERVATIONAL STUDIES OF CONTEMPORARY AND PAST CLIMATES

Observational studies play an important role in three areas: (1) the formulation of ideas and models of how climate operates, (2) the general validation of theories and models, and (3) the construction of climate scenarios.

Studies based on contemporary climatic data have provided a useful starting point for diagnosis of climatic processes that may prove to be relevant to the CO_2 problem. The results of the Global Weather Experiment are now being analyzed and will provide a unique data base for model calibration and validation studies. *Further analyses and diagnostic studies based on contemporary climatic data sets, particularly the Global Weather Experiment data set, should be encouraged.* However, scenarios based on contemporary data sets do not yet provide a firm basis for climatic assessment of possible CO_2-induced climatic changes, nor should they be considered adequate at present for validation of CO_2 sensitivity studies with climate models.

Studies of past climatic data are leading to important advances in climate theory. For example, the large climatic changes between glacial and interglacial periods are being linked with relatively small changes in solar radiation due to variations in the Earth's orbit. If confirmed, these studies will improve our understanding of the sensitivity of climate to small changes in the Earth's radiation budget. A large multidisciplinary effort will be required to acquire the requisite data and carry out the analysis, and such work should be encouraged. Studies of past climate are also potentially valuable because they deal with large changes of the climate system, including the atmosphere, oceans, and cryosphere; because they can reveal regional patterns of climate change; and because there is knowledge of the changes in forcing (now including changes both in atmospheric CO_2 concentrations and in solar radiation) that are apparently driving the system.

DEVELOPMENT OF MONITORING AND EARLY DETECTION STRATEGIES

A comprehensive set of variables should be monitored in order to discriminate CO_2-induced changes from changes in climate caused by other factors. These variables should include CO_2 concentration in the atmosphere, the solar irradiance, the spectral distribution of solar and terrestrial radiation (at the top and bottom of the atmosphere), and concentrations of aerosol and minor constituents in the atmosphere.

A set of indices that have a large signal-to-noise ratio with respect to CO_2-induced changes should be identified and monitored.

Emphasis should be placed on the compilation and analysis of past climatic data to acquire more reliable reconstructions of past variations of climate on a variety of space scales.

The operational monitoring of the ocean's response to climatic change may provide an early indication of climate change. Of particular value appear to be such indices as potential temperature and salinity changes on isopycnals in the wind-driven gyres.

1
Introduction and Overview

It has been known for over a century that trace gases in the atmosphere play a major role in controlling the Earth's heat balance and in maintaining surface temperatures at their current levels. Tyndall (1863) clearly described this "greenhouse" effect, pointing out that water vapor transmits a major fraction of the incident sunlight but strongly absorbs thermal radiation from the Earth. Later, Arrhenius (1896) and Chamberlin (1899) observed that CO_2 also contributes to maintaining the heat balance and that changes in its abundance in the atmosphere could therefore affect the Earth's temperature. Indeed, Arrhenius (1896) estimated that a doubling of atmospheric CO_2 concentrations would produce a global warming of about 6°C. Concern about human influences on CO_2 concentrations and climate was voiced by Callendar (1938). Since then, our understanding of the physical processes governing climate has advanced markedly, but the inference that man-made changes in atmospheric composition can substantially affect climate has remained virtually unchanged. The stubborn refusal of the CO_2 problem to "go away" is in itself significant.

Increasing the sense of urgency is the firmly established observational evidence of steadily increasing CO_2 concentrations in the global atmosphere. These agree within roughly a factor of 2 with estimates of CO_2 emissions from growing fossil-fuel combustion, release of carbon by man from forest and soil reservoirs, and absorption of airborne CO_2 in the oceans and the terrestrial biosphere. Moreover, we have acquired a heightened awareness of the sensitivity of our world society to changes in climate (e.g., World Meteorological Organization, 1979a). Thus, there is a clear need for assessment of the relationships between human activities, the composition of the atmosphere, global climate, and human welfare.

The influence of changes in atmospheric composition on regional climate by a greenhouse effect is readily demonstrable from common experience. For example, we are all aware that in desert regions, temperatures drop rapidly after sunset, while in humid regions the day's heat lingers far into the night. In August, temperatures in Phoenix drop more than 30°F between afternoon and the following dawn; in Washington, the corresponding cooling is less than 20°F. Water vapor, like CO_2, absorbs and re-emits heat radiation strongly, and a moist atmosphere acts as a thermal buffer between the Earth and space. Of course, short-lived local changes in atmospheric moisture or other constituents are not adequate analogs to the long-term global effects of increased CO_2. (This greenhouse effect of water vapor is expected to play an important role in the total warming that might be caused by a rise in atmospheric CO_2: the absorption of heat radiation by CO_2 would increase evaporation and therefore the humidity, leading in turn to additional warming.)

The possibility of climatic changes induced by human activities gained considerable prominence with the increasing postwar awareness of environmental problems. Revelle and Suess (1957) termed man-made injection of CO_2 a "large-scale geophysical experiment," and the President's Science Advisory Committee (1965) report, *Restoring the Quality of Our Environment*, highlighted the CO_2 problem and its potential consequences for the Antarctic Ice Cap. Climatic effects were more closely examined by a group of prominent U.S. scientists at the Study of Critical Environmental Problems (SCEP, 1970), held in preparation for the 1972 United Nations Conference on the Human Environment. This group strongly stated its concern over the potential effects of CO_2 on climate and urged continuing study of the problem and monitoring of atmospheric CO_2. SCEP prompted a more detailed review of the potential for inadvertent climate modification resulting from a wide range of human activities. The Study of Man's Impact on Climate (SMIC, 1971) involved leading scientists from all over the world and gave detailed recommendations on further research and monitoring efforts needed. The global carbon cycle, its possible alterations by man, and the consequent implications for airborne concentrations of CO_2 were addressed at major international workshops (Stumm, 1977; Bolin et al., 1979).

Comprehensive reviews organized in the early 1970's to lay the foundations for national and world climate research programs cited the effect of increased CO_2 on climate as a major research problem (U.S. Committee for the Global Atmospheric Research Program, 1975; Joint Organizing Committee, 1975). In 1977, a National Research Council (NRC) study (Geophysics Study Committee, 1977) concluded that "the climatic effects of carbon dioxide release may be the primary limiting factor on energy production from fossil

Introduction and Overview

fuels over the next few centuries'' and recommended a well-coordinated research program to resolve the uncertainties in our understanding. A *de novo* analysis by a group of independent scientists (JASON, 1979) reinforced the general consensus on the problem's nature and magnitude, while a later study by the same group (JASON, 1980) contributed suggestions for research initiatives and monitoring strategies. At the request of the Office of Science and Technology Policy, reviews of the climate modeling aspects and economic–social implications were conducted (Climate Research Board, 1979, 1980).

The national research program recommended in NRC reports took shape under the aegis of the National Climate Program and the Department of Energy (NOAA, 1980; U.S. Department of Energy, 1979). Internationally, the World Climate Conference (World Meteorological Organization, 1979a) highlighted the CO_2 problem, and its study became a major objective of the World Climate Program. Comprehensive international studies in the context of energy–climate interactions were also conducted at the International Institute for Applied Systems Analysis (Williams, 1978) and the University of Muenster (Bach *et al.*, 1980). Under the auspices of the World Meteorological Organization (WMO), the International Council of Scientific Unions (ICSU), and the United Nations Environment Program (UNEP), an expert group meeting in Villach, Austria, drafted an authoritative document (World Meteorological Organization, 1981), which is expected to form the basis for a coordinated international study effort in the context of the World Climate Program.

The present study seeks to contribute to this continuing process of research, analysis, and assessment by re-examining the issues addressed by the 1979 Charney report in the light of the considerable additional research conducted since its preparation. As in the earlier report, the input to the deliberations was an assumption on the projected loading rate of atmospheric CO_2. This involves not only a prediction of the anthropogenic worldwide production rates but also the role of the climate system (the atmosphere, oceans, cryosphere, and biosphere) in absorbing, transforming, storing, transporting, and interchanging carbonates and other trace constituents, which themselves interact—in short, the complex biogeochemical cycles. These processes are further complicated by the possibility that they, in turn, may be influenced by climatic change and variability. To simplify the working assumptions, we have accepted as the best current estimate of net CO_2 loading rates that which was developed recently by the WMO/ICSU/UNEP group of experts (World Meteorological Organization, 1981): ''. . . the atmospheric CO_2 concentration in 2025 will be between 410 ppm and 490 ppm with a most likely value of 450 ppm.'' However, because of the large number of existing studies addressing the effects of doubled concentrations, we have employed a doubling as a convenient benchmark. In any event, the range of effects between present concentrations and a doubling covers no significant thresholds, and our conclusions are not critically dependent on the detailed time evolution of CO_2 concentrations.

It should be said at the outset that the problem of understanding the climate's response to a given scenario of CO_2 change in the atmosphere is hardly distinguishable from the fundamental problem of understanding the natural variation and change of climate. For this reason, what is currently understood about the CO_2 question is largely the result of progressive developments in climate modeling over the past quarter century. Climate models remain the most powerful means for dealing consistently and quantitatively with the complex system of highly interactive processes that determine climate. Further progress in sharpening our insights and estimates on the CO_2 question, therefore, will continue to depend greatly on our ability to construct more faithful climate models. However, in this report we do not attempt to undertake a comprehensive review of the climate modeling problem itself, that is, such factors as the representation of the planetary boundary layer, the development of more accurate methods for computing radiative transfer, or an accounting for the influence of topographic features on the general circulation and regional climate. Nor do we attempt to catalog existing climate models and their relative performance. Such reviews are to be found elsewhere (e.g., Joint Organizing Committee, 1975, 1979). Our emphasis here is on those modeling problems that we perceive now most specifically to impede our ability to make sounder and more precise judgments on the likely response of the real climate to a given rate of CO_2 increase. We emphasize radiatively connected processes because of the controversy in recent literature, and we specifically discuss a few papers that suggest a lower climate sensitivity.

Quite clearly, the role of the oceans and the cryosphere seems paramount in influencing the nature of the climatic response, particularly in its evolutionary qualities.

The possible interactive role that clouds may play in a shifting climate regime remains one of the unresolved mysteries. The question is how the cloud field would vary in concert with other changes induced by CO_2 and thus alter the radiative transfer in the atmosphere. It is not yet even clear whether systematic cloud changes will provide a net amplification or an attenuation of the climate's sensitivity. Also in connection with the radiation field are the interactive effects of other trace gases and aerosols. Some new results indicate that, at least for the present, they cannot be ignored in addressing the CO_2 question.

Simplified climate models, which approximate only grossly horizontal transport processes, have become a popular tool for CO_2 analysis. We therefore endeavor to delineate their strengths and weaknesses in contrast to the physically more comprehensive, but far more expensive and time-consuming, three-dimensional, time-dependent general-circulation models of the atmosphere and ocean.

The confidence that one can place on the results of climate simulations is calibrated by a model's ability to replicate a variety of known physical states. Since laboratory-based, experimental sources of validation are virtually nonexistent, we must depend on empirical determinations gleaned from the geophysical medium itself. Contemporary climate is one such obvious source, especially its geographical, seasonal, and interannual structure. Furthermore, past climates provide the only records of large excursions in climatic regimes and are a key test-bed for developing and testing climate theory. It is becoming increasingly clear that the major climatic changes of the scale of glacial fluctuations are at least in part produced by the temporal and latitudinal changes of solar radiation brought about by slight changes in the Earth's orbital parameters (obliquity, time of perihelion, eccentricity). This finding promises a major advance in our knowledge of the sensitivity of climate to a small but well-known external forcing change. With both external forcing and climatic changes identified, there is an opportunity to identify and to quantify the role of internal feedbacks. In particular, studies of past climates may be especially germane to the CO_2 question because there is evidence that atmospheric CO_2 itself may have undergone large variations in the past. Often, only limited properties of the climate system of the past can be ascertained. For example, in the case of the last ice age 18,000 years ago, it is primarily the polar-ice perimeter, the sea-surface temperature, and the continental vegetation regimes that can be reconstructed, to a limited extent seasonally, but with limitations both temporally and geographically. Because the state of the climate system is incompletely known, even at present, every attempt must be made to determine the state as completely and with as little ambiguity as possible. We venture here to document the methods of validation and the conclusions that one can draw about the fidelity with which models can at present simulate climate and its variations. Special emphasis is given to the oceans because of their central and only partially understood role.

One of the validation objectives specific to the CO_2 question is the early detection of actual CO_2-induced climatic changes predicted by climate models. Here one wishes to identify a small signal that may be obscured by the background of natural variability. If this variability were understood, it would be internally generated by the climate model and would permit derivation of a signal-to-noise ratio. In this case, the model could be used not only to determine the optimum climatic indices to monitor but also when, where, and how to monitor. However, should the model not incorporate an important climatic process, such as the effects of ubiquitous trace gases or an ability to account for the effects of an extraordinary event such as a volcanic eruption, a monitoring strategy based on model simulations could well be misleading. These questions are discussed in this report.

The end product that is needed to assess the likely impacts of climate change on human activity is a comprehensive picture, or "scenario," of the time–space structure and the amount of that change. The relevant climate indices will depend on the particular activity under consideration. For example, temperature, precipitation, soil moisture, and solar radiation reaching the ground will be germane to an assessment of the impacts of climate change on agriculture. In this report, we address the question of scenario development, with some indication of our present abilities and measures of uncertainty.

Finally, despite the admitted existence of numerous uncertainties, the consensus on the nature and magnitude of the problem has remained remarkably constant throughout this long worldwide process of study and deliberation. Burning of fossil fuels releases to the atmosphere carbon that was extracted by ancient plants many millions of years ago. The most recent projections of future energy consumption suggest a slackening in the growth in energy consumption; nevertheless, even the most conservative estimates imply major CO_2 injections. The details of the natural carbon cycle and the future disposition of injected CO_2 are still unclear, but it seems certain that much man-made CO_2 will remain in the atmosphere. Although questions have been raised about the magnitude of climatic effects, no one denies that changes in atmospheric CO_2 concentration have the potential to influence the heat balance of the Earth and atmosphere. Finally, although possibly beneficial effects on biological photosynthetic productivity have been recognized, no one denies that an altered climate would to some extent influence how humanity secures its continuing welfare.

This report addresses the uncertainties in but one element of this consensus: the effects of changed concentrations of airborne CO_2 on global climate. Other questions will be similarly studied in the course of a comprehensive NRC study of the entire issue, which is to be conducted over the next several years.

2
Principal Scientific Issues in Modeling Studies

GLOBAL CLIMATE SENSITIVITY—SIMPLIFIED MODELS AND EMPIRICAL APPROACHES

The sensitivity of climate to changes in CO_2 concentrations has been examined through two apparently different approaches: (1) by climate models that account for the energy-balance components of the complete surface–atmosphere system and (2) from empirical observations keyed to the surface energy balance alone.

Simplified climate models, ranging from zero-dimensional empirical relationships to highly parameterized multidimensional models, can be useful for inexpensive studies of climate change and climate mechanisms over a wide range of time scales, if used with appropriate caution. The basic strength of these models is that they permit economically feasible analyses over a wide range of parameter space. Such studies are valuable for focusing and interpreting studies performed with more complex and realistic global models. However, it must be realized that the simplified models are limited in the information they can provide on local or regional climate change. Such detailed inferences can be obtained from three-dimensional general-circulation models (3-D GCM's) of the type discussed in the Charney report and in the section Model Studies and from empirical studies, although both approaches are severely limited in current capabilities.

One-Dimensional Models

The one-dimensional (i.e., treating a vertical column through the atmosphere) radiative–convective (1-D RC) models provide a good illustration of the use

TABLE 2.1 Equilibrium Surface Temperature Increase Due to Doubled CO_2 (300 ppm → 600 ppm) in 1-D RC Models [a,b]

Model	Description[c]	ΔT_s (°C)	f	F (W m^{-2})
1	FAH, 6.5LR, FCA	1.2	1	4.0
2	FRH, 6.5LR, FCA	1.9	1.6	3.9
3	Same as 2, except MALR replaces 6.5LR	1.4	0.7	4.0
4	Same as 2, except FCT replaces FCA	2.8	1.4	3.9
5	Same as 2, except SAF included[d]	2.5–2.8	1.3–1.4	
6	Same as 2, except VAF included[e]	~ 3.5	~ 1.8	

[a] Data from Hansen et al., 1981.
[b] Model 1 has no feedbacks affecting the atmosphere's radiative properties. The feedback factor f specifies the impact of each added process on model sensitivity to doubled CO_2. F is the equilibrium thermal flux into the planetary surface if the ocean temperature is held fixed (infinite heat capacity) when CO_2 is doubled; this is the flux after the atmosphere has adjusted to the radiative perturbation within the model constraints indicated but before the surface temperature has increased.
[c] FRH, fixed relative humidity; FAH, fixed absolute humidity; 6.5LR, 6.5°C km^{-1} limiting lapse rate; MALR, moist adiabatic limiting lapse rate; FCA, fixed cloud altitude; FCT, fixed cloud temperature; SAF, snow–ice albedo feedback; VAF, vegetation albedo feedback.
[d] Based on Wang and Stone, 1980.
[e] Based on Cess, 1978.

of simplified models. For example, the basic greenhouse mechanism by which atmospheric CO_2 warms the Earth can be analyzed with the help of such models. Indeed, the sensitivity of the surface temperature in 1-D RC models to changes in CO_2 amount is in general agreement with the sensitivity of more realistic 3-D GCM's, suggesting that 1-D RC models are able to simulate certain basic mechanisms and feedbacks in 3-D GCM's. It is thus of value to use a 1-D RC model to illustrate processes that influence climate-model equilibrium sensitivity and also to compare the results of these models to observed climate variations.

The main processes known to influence climate-model sensitivity are summarized in Table 2.1 (Hansen et al., 1981). Note that the change in equilibrium global-mean temperature, "equilibrium sensitivity," deduced from 1-D RC models is of the order of 1°C for doubled CO_2, even in the absence of feedback effects. The increase in atmospheric water vapor that

Principal Scientific Issues in Modeling Studies

occurs with rising temperature increases the sensitivity to almost 2°C for doubled CO_2. The atmospheric lapse rate (vertical temperature gradient) may also change in response to increasing atmospheric temperature and water vapor. At low latitudes, where the lapse rate is nearly moist adiabatic, this represents a negative feedback, while more stable lapse rates at high latitudes lead to a positive feedback on surface temperature. A positive cloud feedback occurs if clouds move to higher altitude with increasing temperature, but changes in cloud cover may lead to either a positive or a negative feedback. Improved empirical data on clouds and better modeling capabilities are needed to evaluate cloud effects. Ice–snow albedo feedback is clearly positive. Preliminary estimates of vegetation albedo feedback are also positive but very uncertain.

The sensitivity of the global-mean temperature in simplified climate models to increased atmospheric CO_2 is consistent with that found with 3-D GCM's, i.e., 3 ± 1.5°C (see the section Model Studies).

Surface Energy Balance Considerations

The surface energy balance approach has been adopted in a number of studies of climate sensitivity applied to the CO_2 problem (Callendar, 1938; Plass, 1956a, 1956b; Kaplan, 1960; Möller, 1963; Newell and Dopplick, 1979; Idso, 1980a; Kandel, 1981). Manabe and Wetherald (1967) discussed the difficulties in attempting to estimate global surface temperature response to increased CO_2 from consideration of surface energy balance. They demonstrated that the complete surface–atmosphere energy balance must be considered to obtain valid results.

Two recent studies (Newell and Dopplick, 1979; Idso, 1980a) yielded a CO_2-induced surface warming substantially smaller than the warming obtained from the studies of the complete surface–atmosphere system. On closer examination, it is found that there is no basic disagreement between the empirical evidence used in these studies and the climate-model results. Indeed, the empirical response data provide some valuable tests of the models. Below we provide a summary discussion of how increased CO_2 modifies the radiation and energy balance of the complete surface–atmosphere system. In the following section we briefly discuss some of the dissenting inferences of surface-temperature sensitivity. More detailed discussion of aspects of the surface energy balance are given by Ramanathan (1981).

Models of the Earth's Complete Energy Balance

Numerical climate models treat the energy balance of the complete surface–atmosphere system. For the purposes of the present discussion, it is sufficient to focus on but two components of the system—the troposphere and the surface—because the stratosphere's role in the energy balance is relatively small. For example, in the case of doubled CO_2, inclusion of the stratosphere and thus the downward infrared flux from the stratosphere into the troposphere would increase the calculated total radiative energy flux into the troposphere by only about 30 percent (Schneider, 1975; Ramanathan et al., 1979). This stratospheric effect is included in most climate-model studies and in the estimates of CO_2 heating given later in this report. On time scales longer than several weeks, the troposphere is closely coupled to the surface, particularly on a global-mean basis. The principal processes responsible for this coupling are the exchange of latent, sensible, and radiative heat fluxes between the air and the surface through the boundary layer and the horizontal and vertical convective processes within the troposphere. Because of vertical mixing, in particular, the response of the global-mean temperature of the troposphere and surface depends primarily on the heating perturbation to the surface–troposphere system *as a whole* and is relatively insensitive to the vertical distribution of the perturbation heating within the system. This conclusion has been reinforced in a series of GCM experiments (Manabe and Wetherald, 1975; Wetherald and Manabe, 1975) in which comparable surface–tropospheric heating perturbations due to increases in both CO_2 and solar constant produced similar surface-temperature responses, even though the vertical distribution of heating was significantly different.

For a doubling of CO_2, radiative calculations show that the surface–troposphere system is subjected to a net radiative heating of about 4 W m^{-2} before any adjustments in temperature or other climatic variables are allowed to occur. Roughly 2.5 W m^{-2} of this heating is caused by a reduction in the outgoing infrared radiation from the surface–troposphere system, and most of the remaining heating is due to an increase in the downward infrared emission by the stratosphere (Schneider, 1975; Ramanathan et al., 1979; Hansen et al., 1981). As summarized in the Charney report and in the section One-Dimensional Models, most climate models translate this radiative heating into a warming of the surface equilibrium temperature by about 1 K if the amount of water vapor in the atmosphere is held fixed. This value increases to about 2 K as a result of the increased water vapor abundances expected to accompany increasing atmospheric temperatures, a positive feedback included in most climate models.

Dissenting Inferences from Energy-Balance Models and Empirical Studies

Inferences of a relatively small sensitivity of climate to changes in CO_2 have been made recently (Newell and Dopplick, 1979; Idso, 1980a, 1980b, 1981).

Principal Scientific Issues in Modeling Studies 19

These papers are based on incomplete methods or observations, and their conclusions appear to be of limited utility in assessing the climatic effects of increased CO_2.

As indicated above, the sensitivity of climate to a perturbation in some radiative process can best be assessed by considering the entire global Earth–atmosphere system. Approaches centered on the surface, limited regions, or time-limited observations necessarily become more complex because many fluxes and reservoirs of energy must be explicitly and quantitatively taken into account. In determining the effects of increased atmospheric CO_2 on the surface, a number of effects are produced by a group of interconnected processes:

1. Additional heating of the surface due to additional radiation from the atmosphere;
2. Reduced cooling of the troposphere due to reduction of radiative heat emission from the troposphere to space;
3. Heating of the surface by additional radiation from a warmer troposphere;
4. Increases in sensible and latent heat fluxes from the surface to the atmosphere, thus moderating the surface-temperature increase, heating the atmosphere, and increasing atmospheric moisture;
5. Increased heating of the troposphere by increased absorption of solar radiation by increased water vapor (and CO_2);
6. Increased heating of the surface due to enhanced radiation from the additional moisture in the atmosphere;
7. Exchanges of sensible and latent heat with regions not explicitly treated; and (in nonequilibrium cases)
8. Thermal inertia of the land surface, the atmosphere, and especially the oceans.

All of these processes must be taken into account in calculating new equilibrium conditions for the surface and atmosphere in which increased net radiative heating of the surface is balanced by increased net fluxes of sensible and latent heat from the surface and to other regions. It is within this context that we consider the cited studies.

Idso compares several sets of empirical observations of changes in downward radiative flux at the surface with corresponding changes in surface temperature. From each case, he computes an empirical "response function" relating a change in downward radiative flux to a change in surface temperature. He finds the values of this parameter to be virtually constant among the cases he considers. He then estimates from a radiation model the change in downward flux that would result from doubling atmospheric CO_2 concentration and employs the empirical response function to calculate a rather small surface-temperature change. This approach is misleading when applied to estimation of the response of global-mean equilibrium climate to increased CO_2:

1. It is clear that the response function can be calculated quite arbitrarily at virtually any value in nonequilibrium situations, according to the choice of data. For example, surface temperatures rise between noon and midafternoon and between June and July (in the northern hemisphere), although in both cases, incident solar radiation decreases; a negative response function might be implied by one of Idso's methods.

2. Some of the "natural experiments" that Idso employs are on time and space scales clearly inappropriate to the CO_2 problem and do not involve the components of the climate system that are important for long-term climate changes. The thermal inertia of the Earth's surface, particularly the 70 percent that is ocean, slows the response of surface temperature to changes in incident radiation. Thus, the observations of temperature changes from day to day or season to season employed by Idso do not reflect the full temperature change that would be experienced at equilibrium if the radiation change were to persist for extended periods. For this reason, the response functions calculated by Idso are necessarily too small for estimation of the equilibrium climatic response to increased CO_2.

3. Idso's interpretation of empirical radiation measurements confuses primary forcing and the amplifying feedbacks engendered by that forcing.

(a) For example, he compares changes in temperature between winter and summer with corresponding changes in solar radiation received at the surface. However, the increase of surface temperature between winter and summer not only results from the primary change in forcing (increased insolation) but also reflects the additional thermal radiation to the surface due to consequent increases in atmospheric temperature and humidity. Thus, in this case, the primary forcing is correctly identified, and some feedbacks are incompletely included in the response.

(b) In another case, Idso (1981) compares the temperature of an airless Earth heated by solar radiation alone with that of today's Earth, which receives energy from both the sun and the atmosphere. Here, however, the true initial forcing would be the hypothetical effect of imposing on rather cool, airless Earth a correspondingly cool but radiatively active atmosphere. The radiation from our present warmer and wetter atmosphere is considerably greater than this conceptual initial forcing, reflecting powerful amplifying feedback processes, and thus represents a mixture of cause and effect. Failure to distinguish clearly and consistently between cause and effect permits erroneous and virtually arbitrary conclusions to be drawn.

The empirical phenomena described by Idso are in fact perfectly consistent with the climate models employed for assessment of CO_2 increases. For example, the seasonal cycles of radiation and temperature have been used with success by a number of modelers for empirical validation (e.g., Warren and Schneider, 1979; North and Coakley, 1979; Manabe and Stouffer, 1980; Hansen et al., 1981).

Newell and Dopplick (1979) deal with the effect of doubled CO_2 in the tropics, primarily the effect on the temperature of the tropical ocean. Holding atmospheric parameters fixed, they calculate an increase in energy received at the surface due to doubled CO_2. Using formulas for transfer of sensible, latent, and radiative energy from the surface, they estimate a relatively small temperature increase for the tropical ocean. Somewhat larger increases are computed for tropical land areas. They estimate the change in the surface energy budget produced by the increased atmospheric moisture (resulting from the assumed enhanced evaporation) to be about as large as the initial change due to CO_2, doubling the effect of the CO_2 itself. Nevertheless, they project only a very small increase in low-latitude surface temperatures. As corroboration, they cite the small temperature changes observed after the 1963 Mt. Agung eruption, which produced an increase in stratospheric aerosols and a decrease in solar energy received at the surface. Newell and Dopplick (1981) have also called attention to paleoclimatic data indicating that tropical ocean temperatures have varied but little in the past, although CO_2 concentrations are known to have changed.

As suggested above, the temperature of the Earth's surface is maintained by a balance between fluxes of sensible, latent, and radiant energy between the surface and the overlying atmosphere. The effect of a perturbation in one component of these fluxes can be evaluated correctly only by a complete, internally consistent, and energy-conserving treatment. The Newell–Dopplick arguments are faulty in this respect. To begin with, they treat the tropics in isolation, without considering the exchange of energy with higher latitudes. Moreover,

1. They fail to take into account satisfactorily the effects of atmospheric changes that would accompany CO_2 increase. For example:

(a) Newell and Dopplick employ formulas expressing fluxes of sensible and latent heat from the surface in terms of differences in temperature and vapor pressure between the surface and the near-surface air. They estimate the sensitivity of surface temperature to increased CO_2 by calculating the increase of surface temperature needed to increase heat fluxes from the surface sufficiently to counterbalance the additional energy input from the atmosphere, *while holding atmospheric temperature and absolute humidity fixed*. In reality, surface temperature and near-surface air conditions are closely coupled by means of these same fluxes, so that a given change in surface temperature gives rise to a much smaller change in the magnitude of the air–surface differences. Thus, their assumption overestimates the magnitude of changes in air–surface differences and consequently also overestimates the magnitude of surface-air fluxes associated with a change in surface temperature. For this reason, they erroneously conclude that only a small increase in surface temperature would be required to enhance upward fluxes from the surface and balance CO_2-induced downward fluxes. In reality, the surface warming is accompanied by increases in the temperature and absolute humidity of the overlying air. Therefore, a much larger increase of surface temperature would be required to balance the surface energy budget. Thus, it is not difficult to appreciate why Newell and Dopplick indicate an extremely small sensitivity of surface temperature to an increase in atmospheric CO_2 concentration.

(b) The radiative effect of increased atmospheric moisture appears to be greatly underestimated, probably because the moisture and temperature of the air column are not allowed to come completely into equilibrium with the surface.

2. The Mt. Agung observations are, in fact, not inconsistent with the results of models used for estimating climatic sensitivity to increased CO_2 (Pollack *et al.*, 1976; Mass and Schneider, 1977; Hansen *et al.*, 1978, 1981). It would be expected that the heat capacity of the ocean would slow the response, causing the temperature change experienced during the brief residence period of the aerosol to be but a fraction of that which would be realized at equilibrium (Hansen *et al.*, 1978; Hoffert *et al.*, 1980). However, the limited observations of stratospheric aerosol optical depth and the lack of data on quantitative heating properties of aerosols suggest that the Mt. Agung observations cannot be taken as definitive indications of climatic sensitivity.

Thus, the results of Newell and Dopplick on the tropical surface energy balance do not refute the inferences of a global climate sensitivity obtained from comprehensive models of the complete global climate system.

Questions of a different character were raised by Lindzen *et al.* (1982), who employed a cumulus convective parameterization in a 1-D RC model. They obtained a sensitivity to CO_2 increase about 35 percent smaller than that with their model using fixed-lapse-rate convective adjustment. This conclusion is in close agreement with the results of similar model experiments presented in Table 2.1; use of a moist adiabatic lapse rate in Model 2 in order to reflect cumulus convective processes produces a sensitivity that is smaller than that indicated by Model 2 with fixed lapse rate. Similarly, global 3-D GCM's also show a relatively small sensitivity in the tropics, where cumulus convective processes are strong and moist adiabatic lapse rates

Principal Scientific Issues in Modeling Studies

prevail (Manabe and Stouffer, 1980). The response of global-mean temperature is, of course, influenced strongly by the relatively large temperature increases projected for higher latitudes, where cumulus convective processes are less important. Thus, a careful comparison of Lindzen *et al*. results with available 1-D (with moist-lapse-rate adjustment) and 3-D climate models suggests that the overall magnitude of the CO_2 warming does not depend greatly on the details of the convective parameterization employed, although that component of the models is one of many that warrant more careful study.

The preceding discussion clearly illustrates the complex nature of the surface energy budget and the dangers involved in inferring global climate sensitivity from local surface observations. However, empirical methods of inferring sensitivity are appealing. The real value of empirical studies is that they are necessary to verify the behavior of climate models. A promising empirical method has been proposed by Cess (1976), who obtains sensitivity estimates from the latitudinal gradient in annually and zonally averaged radiation budgets as obtained from satellite radiation measurements and obtains surface-temperature responses consistent with climate-model studies.

To summarize, the sensitivity of climate to increased CO_2 obtained from most global climate model studies is entirely consistent with the inferences drawn from surface energy balance studies and empirical approaches, *provided* that the latter methods account fully for the globally connected energy budget and transport processes within the entire surface–atmosphere system on the appropriate time scales.

Some of the important implications of the global sensitivity analysis are summarized below:

1. Because of the strong coupling between the surface and the troposphere, the global-mean surface warming is driven by the CO_2 radiative heating of the entire surface–troposphere system and not *only* by the direct CO_2 radiative heating at the surface.

2. The magnitude of the surface–troposphere warming is determined by horizontal advective and vertical convective–radiative interactions between the atmosphere and surface (in particular, the oceans).

3. Some recent studies of the climatic effects of increased CO_2 based on the surface energy balance approach have not fully accounted for the processes described in points 1 and 2 above. When these limitations are taken into account, their results are seen to be entirely consistent with those of comprehensive models. However, inconsistent interpretation of incomplete analyses can yield virtually arbitrary conclusions (cf. Möller, 1963).

4. Empirical approaches to estimating climate sensitivity from observations should be encouraged, since they may provide a valuable source for calibrating

or validating model results. However, such approaches should emphasize global-scale measurements and also should infer sensitivity from natural climate change "experiments" in which long-term ocean–atmosphere interactions are involved in the climate change. Satellite radiation budget measurements should be a valuable data base for such endeavors.

ROLE OF THE OCEANS

Role of the Ocean in the Transient Response of Climate

The Charney report emphasized a significant but relatively unexplored question about the role of the oceans in the climate system. The heat capacity of the upper ocean is potentially great enough to delay for several decades the establishment of new equilibrium temperatures associated with increased atmospheric CO_2, with consequent impact both on social implications and on verification strategies. The dominant effect of a sudden doubling of atmospheric CO_2, in the absence of ocean warming, would be a net downward flux of heat at the ocean surface of about 4 W m^{-2} and an almost imperceptible change in atmospheric temperature over most of the globe (Ramanathan, 1981). If this heat flux were maintained indefinitely, a well-mixed layer 50 m deep would warm to a new equilibrium temperature 2°C higher in 3 years, whereas one 500 m deep would take 30 years, and the involvement of the whole ocean, 5000 m deep on average, would take 300 years. (In reality, of course, the net flux is partially compensated by increased fluxes of sensible and latent heat from the ocean to the atmosphere, and the approach to equilibrium is still further delayed.) To what depth would mixing take place before a significant rise in sea-surface temperatures takes place? This question is fundamental and quite distinct from the ocean's role in moderating the rise in atmospheric CO_2 concentration itself.

Few relevant studies have been published. Manabe and Stouffer (1980) used a physically comprehensive GCM of the atmosphere but a simple oceanic mixed layer of about 70-m depth to simulate the annual cycle. However, in the absence of a deeper ocean, this model was insufficient to describe a longer-term approach toward a new equilibrium. Schneider and Thompson (1981) combined a simplified atmospheric model with a two-box model of the ocean and predicted that 25 percent of the increase in surface temperature following an instantaneous doubling of CO_2 would be delayed by at least 20 years. They also suggest that the evolution of the latitudinal temperature contrast would be significantly affected.

Although the mechanisms for vertical exchange in the oceans are only

Principal Scientific Issues in Modeling Studies

qualitatively understood and are difficult to model reliably, certain broad statements can be made with confidence, which indicate the general nature and probable magnitude of the oceans' role in moderating climatic change. Preliminary assumptions and arguments are presented here as a framework for future discussion and research.

The most important assumption is controversial. It is that within the ocean itself an increment of heat behaves approximately as a passive tracer, i.e., it does not substantially alter the exchange processes that transfer it downward. In general, this dynamical assertion is certainly false, but it is relatively plausible in the upper ocean, where vertical mixing is driven predominantly by the wind and seasonal overturning and where the horizontal circulation is due mainly to wind stress rather than gradients in surface temperature.

The nature of these exchange processes may be inferred from observations of other tracers in the ocean. For example, Figure 2.1 shows the distribution of tritium as determined by the GEOSECS (1973–1974) cruises along a section in the western Pacific from Antarctica to Alaska, approximately 10 years after the tritium was deposited at the surface, predominantly in the northern hemisphere during a 3-year period around 1964 (Fine *et al.*, 1981). Tritium is a passive tracer, both dynamically and chemically. It is apparent that penetration had already occurred to a depth of 700 m in both hemispheres in mid-latitudes and to a depth of 300 m in the tropics, with the upper two thirds of this volume being of approximately uniform concentration within each hemisphere. Isopleths of constant concentration also coincide to a considerable degree with surfaces of constant potential density. This is consistent with the widely, though not universally, accepted view that below a surface-wind-mixed layer and a seasonal thermocline, which is some 50 m deep in the tropics and 200–300 m deep in mid-latitudes, the dominant exchange processes in the ocean are by quasi-horizontal circulation and lateral mixing on surfaces of constant potential density of water with wintertime surface characteristics. This isopycnal exchange (i.e., lateral on potential density surfaces) leads to ventilation of the remaining volume down to 1000 m. The ventilation time increases with depth, but in the upper few hundred meters it is at most a few years. A corresponding tritium section in the Atlantic shows similar features, except that in addition there is entrainment into the abyssal water north of 50° N.

There are many pathways whereby a tracer such as tritium, or heat, can be carried downward from the ocean surface, and many reservoirs in which it can accumulate. However, as the concentration in a reservoir builds up, some of the tracer-enriched water is returned to the surface, and that reservoir becomes saturated. Pathways to deeper and larger reservoirs remain active. Thus, the volume of water reached by such pathways is an increasing function of time, but after a long time the specifics of the near-surface pathways are

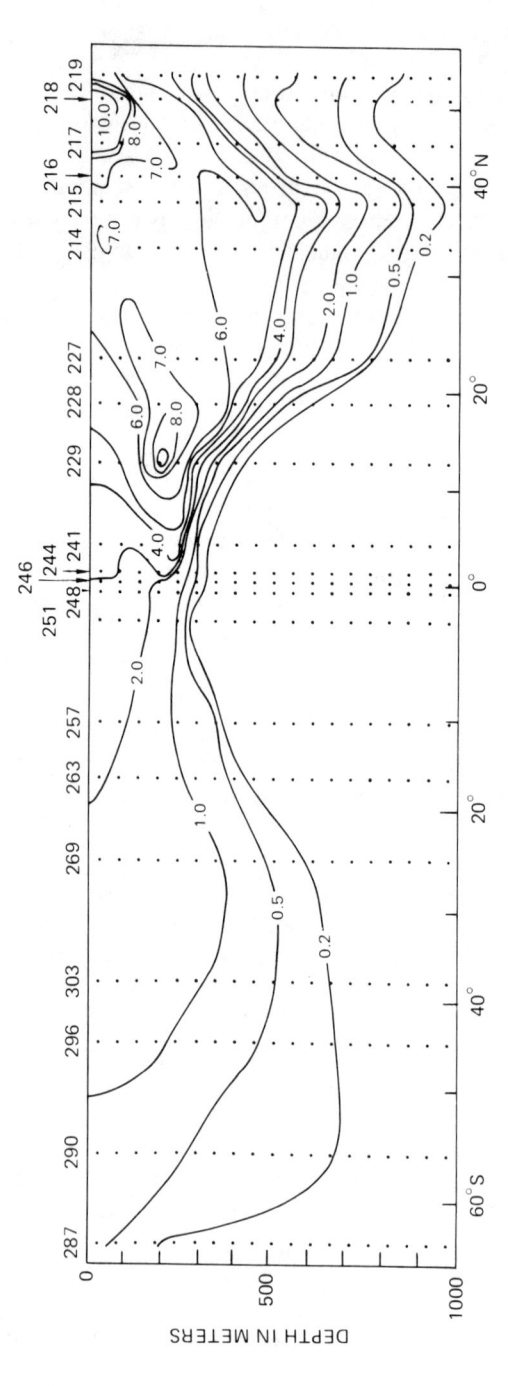

FIGURE 2.1 North–south vertical section of tritium (TU) along the western GEOSECS (1973–1974) Pacific track (from the Aleutian Islands to 69° S) between 165° W and 170° E. Although the series of nuclear tests in the early 1960's increased the global tritium inventory by an order of magnitude over that from the mid-1950's tests, the contribution from the early tests cannot be ignored. Water containing tritium can therefore be assumed to have been in contact with the atmosphere in, at most, the 17 years prior to GEOSECS (Fine et al., 1981).

Principal Scientific Issues in Modeling Studies 27

unimportant, provided they are efficient enough to transmit the fluxes necessary to fill the deeper reservoirs. The accumulation time can be roughly estimated from the volume of specific reservoirs and the supposed exchange rates of water between them. For a time scale of a few weeks, the relevant volume is to a depth of 10–100 m because of wind-induced vertical mixing. On a time scale of 1 year, it is to the base of the seasonal thermocline, around 50 m in the tropics and 200–300 m in mid-latitude. The tritium data show that on a time scale of 10 years, the volume is to a globally averaged equivalent depth of about 500 m, access to most of that probably being through the surface layers poleward of 45° N and 45° S. On a time scale of 1000 years, the whole world ocean is involved (Munk, 1966), with an average depth of 5000 m.

These time scales are for downward mixing. The feedback of a rise of surface temperature on the downward flux of heat at the surface must also be considered. The surface heat flux into the ocean decreases as the surface temperature rises toward a new equilibrium. The rate of rise of the surface temperature depends on the depth to which mixing takes place. As pointed out earlier, typical thermal time constants are 3 years for a 50-m-deep mixed layer, 30 years for a layer 500 m thick, and 300 years for 5000 m. Near the surface, the thermal time constant is much greater than the mixing time, allowing a thermal anomaly to penetrate with little negative feedback on surface heating. On the other hand, the ventilation time of the abyssal waters is substantially longer than the corresponding thermal time constant, implying that the exchanges with deep waters are relatively minor contributions to the heat budget of the layers above. Thus the main thermocline will remain more closely coupled to the atmosphere above than the abyssal water below. Unfortunately, the crossover between these extremes occurs at intermediate depths near the base of the main thermocline, where the ventilation times are relatively poorly known. From tritium and other data, Jenkins (1980) has estimated ventilation times in the Sargasso Sea equal to a few years above 700 m, about 50 years between 700 and 1500 m, and much longer below. It is not known how applicable these estimates may be to other oceans.

The atmospheric effects of CO_2 would be perceived by the ocean as a sudden change in downward heat flux at the ocean surface, as a change in wind stress, and as a change in net evaporation minus precipitation. Although variations in wind stress can substantially alter the circulation in the ocean, and hence the surface temperature, the changes calculated from atmospheric models appear to be small. Net evaporation minus precipitation affects the salinity of surface waters. In high latitudes, the latter controls whether winter cooling leads to deep convective overturning, with associated renewal of the abyssal waters, which comprise four fifths of the volume of the ocean, or to the formation of sea ice, which happens if the surface water is relatively

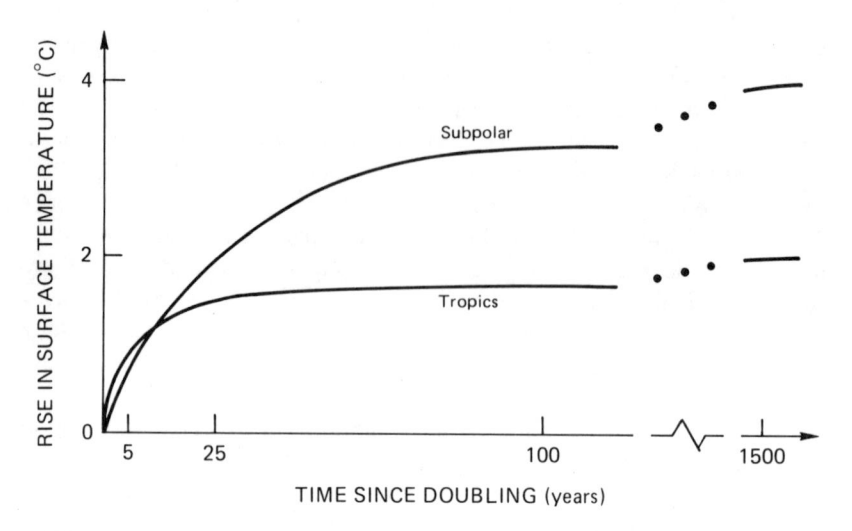

FIGURE 2.2 Schematic representation of the time-dependent response of ocean-surface temperatures in the tropics and subpolar regions to an instantaneous doubling of atmospheric CO_2 sustained indefinitely.

fresh. However, since the present rate of renewal of abyssal water is relatively slow, believed to be once per 1000 years, salinity is probably not of dominant importance for the heat budget of the surface layers, except perhaps indirectly through its influence on the extent of sea ice. Attention will be concentrated here on the direct effects of an increased downward surface heat flux of about 4 W m^{-2}.

A quantitative treatment of these concepts requires at least consideration of a set of reservoirs at different latitudes, coupled in series and parallel according to the picture of oceanic mixing outlined above, to a simplified atmospheric model capable of distinguishing different latitude belts.

It is assumed that for the small changes from present climate that are under consideration, perturbations may be superimposed in an approximately linear manner. This implies that the effects of an arbitrary rise curve in atmospheric CO_2 can be inferred once the ocean response to any particular time sequence has been fully analyzed. For definiteness, consider an instantaneous doubling, maintained thereafter. The qualitative nature of the conclusions from the conceptual model described above is indicated in Figure 2.2. The curves show the rise in ocean-surface temperature in the tropics and in the subpolar regions (45–60° latitude) as a function of time after a hypothetical doubling of atmospheric CO_2. After 1500 years, equilibrium has been reached, with a rise of about 2°C in the tropics and 4°C in subpolar regions. After 5 years,

Principal Scientific Issues in Modeling Studies

the temperature in the tropics has risen significantly—about 50 percent—toward the equilibrium value, but thereafter the rise is much slower, being 80 percent complete after 100 years. In subpolar regions, the initial rate of rise is much slower, being 50 percent complete after 25 years. The decrease in poleward temperature gradient predicted by Manabe and Stouffer (1980) is thus delayed by several decades.

The precise numbers shown in this diagram are clearly dependent on the detailed model under consideration. The general shape of the curves and the orders of magnitude are not. The relatively higher equilibrium rises in high latitudes are prescribed by a number of processes as described in the calculations of Manabe and Stouffer (1980). Possible additional effects due to sustained poleward transport of heat by ocean currents are not included. That 25–50 years is required to achieve most of the equilibrium rise in temperate latitudes is a consequence of the rapid downward exchange there, which is well documented by the tritium data. This rise time is substantially shorter in the tropics because on time scales of 1–3 years the upper 50-m layer is largely isolated from the remainder of the ocean, enabling partial equilibration to be achieved. The equilibration is not complete because of heat transfers to other latitude bands, primarily through the atmosphere but to some extent by near-surface ocean currents, and the short-term fractional rise depends on the efficiency assumed for each of these processes. Even after 100 years, the surface layers as a whole have not come to equilibrium because of the slow transfer of heat downward to abyssal depths, both by water sinking in polar regions and by cold water rising elsewhere. Because of uncertainties about the effective rate of such exchange, an estimate of the fraction of the temperature rise that is delayed 100 years or longer must be regarded as very tentative. Regarding heat as a passive tracer is particularly suspect in this case.

The discussion so far has been entirely in terms of the transient response to an instantaneous but maintained doubling of atmospheric CO_2, which is a highly implausible scenario. However, because of the linearity of the climate system to small perturbations, the response for any other rise curve is readily calculated by convolution of the curves shown in Figure 2.2 (or their more refined equivalent) with the instantaneous equilibrium temperature increase (roughly proportional to the logarithm of the atmospheric CO_2 divided by the base value). For example, if a particular atmospheric CO_2 rise curve scenario implies an equilibrium surface-temperature rise of 3°C in the subpolar regions by A.D. 2050, the actual surface-temperature response can be estimated by the history of the rise by using curves like those shown schematically in Figure 2.2. The rise in equilibrium temperature can be approximated by a finite number of step increases. The actual response of surface temperature in 2050 may then be estimated as the following sum: a large fraction of increases in equilibrium temperature before A.D. 2000, about half of increases between A.D. 2000 and 2030, and a small fraction of increases after A.D. 2030. In the tropics the same principles would apply.

On the basis of the assumption that tracers can serve as an approximate guide, we conclude that the mixing time scale for the main thermocline is less than the thermal time scale associated with increasing CO_2. The waters of the upper thermocline will be closely coupled to the atmosphere on time scales of 1–2 decades. Any estimate of the time response of the climate system to increasing CO_2 will have to take into consideration the thermal inertia of the upper thermocline.

The ocean thermal response may also cause important regional differences in response other than the latitudinal effects already discussed. For example, the geometry of the ocean–land distribution will be important. The climatic response in areas downwind from major oceans will certainly be different from that in the interior of major continents. It is also reasonable to infer that the much smaller ratio of land to sea area in the southern hemisphere will be significant. Depending on how efficiently the atmosphere exchanges heat across the equator, a slower response to increasing CO_2 might be expected in the southern hemisphere. Future modeling studies should stress the regional nature of oceanic thermal inertia, and atmospheric energy transfer mechanisms, taking into account that the local response time is proportional to the ocean's thermal inertia and the rate at which energy is exchanged with the atmosphere.

Reliable quantitative estimates of the role of the ocean in the climate system will require a better understanding of the processes that give rise to the entire general circulation in the ocean and substantial improvements in our ability to model it. Progress to this end must be based on a broad range of research: continued oceanographic observations of density distributions, tracers, heat fluxes and currents, quantitative elucidation of the mixing process, substantial theoretical effort, and the development of models adequate to reproduce the relative magnitudes of a variety of competing effects. The problems are difficult, and complete success is unlikely to come quickly. Meanwhile, partially substantiated assumptions like those asserted here are likely to remain an integral part of any assessment.

In planning the oceanographic field experiments in connection with the World Climate Research Program, we recommend that particular attention be paid to improving estimates of mixing time scales in the main thermocline.

Effects of Sea Ice

Sea ice has profound effects on climate in several ways. In winter, it allows the ocean to remain at the freezing point while the air temperature falls to much lower values. In summer, sea-ice melting locks the surface temperature to the melting point. Manabe and Stouffer (1980) have noted the effect of sea ice on the seasonal dependence of the sensitivity of climate to CO_2 increases. They have shown how the existence of melting sea ice and the large thermal inertia of the ocean's mixed layer prevent the summer temperatures in a high-CO_2 climate from rising much above present levels. Bolin (1981) has recently pointed out that the vertical exchange processes in Antarctic waters ". . . are large in magnitude and are crucial for a proper understanding of the global CO_2 exchange between the atmosphere and the sea. . . ." The role of the Arctic Ocean halocline (Aagard et al., 1981) may also be important in the vertical exchange processes of heat, salt, and CO_2. At high latitudes, warming must be confined to the winter season, when CO_2-induced reductions of sea-ice thickness result in the increase of upward heat conduction through ice. Sea ice also has an important role in the formation of deep water. Ice may be frozen in one location and carried by currents to melt in another location; this process is important for creating cold, salty water that descends to great depths. However, present knowledge of the interaction of ice formation and deep-water formation is still rudimentary. In particular, the relative importance of atmospheric radiation and oceanic mixing processes to the different seasonal sea-ice variations in the northern and southern hemispheres need to be explored. Thus, it will be difficult to say even qualitatively what role sea ice will play in high-latitude response and deep-water formation until the climatic factors that control the areal extent of polar pack ice in the northern and southern hemispheres are known. Field experiments are required to gain fundamental observational data concerning these processes.

CLOUD EFFECTS

Cloudiness–Radiation Feedback

Two uncertain aspects of cloudiness–radiation feedback must be considered. The first is the question of whether cloud amounts, heights, optical properties, and structure will significantly change in response to CO_2-induced warming. If such changes are not significant, then obviously there will be no cloudiness–radiation feedback. But if cloud amounts, types (e.g., cumiliform versus stratiform), heights, optical properties, and structure are influenced by climatic change, then both the solar and the infrared component of the radiation budget will be altered; it is the relative role of these probably small changes and their regional distributions that constitutes the second uncertain aspect of the problem.

If, for example, cloud amounts decrease, then, since cloudy regions are generally brighter than clear-sky regions, the decrease would reduce the planetary albedo, resulting in increased solar heating of the surface–atmosphere system. But decreased cloudiness would also reduce the infrared opacity of the atmosphere, resulting in increased infrared cooling of the surface–atmosphere system. Thus, the separate solar and infrared modifications act in opposite directions. A corresponding change in effective cloud height would further modify the outgoing infrared radiation, with infrared cooling being enhanced, for example, by a reduction in effective cloud height, since the lower (and hence warmer) clouds would radiate more energy to space.

Employing a GCM that predicts both cloud amount and cloud height, Manabe and Wetherald (1980) have, for doubling and quadrupling of atmospheric CO_2, suggested that equatorward of 50° latitude, net cloud amount and effective cloud height are reduced by CO_2-induced warming, with both effects acting to increase the outgoing infrared radiation. However, this is nearly compensated within their model by the corresponding increase in absorbed solar radiation due to reduced cloud amount. Poleward of 50° latitude they find an increase in net cloud amount without any substantial change in effective cloud height. The absence of changes in cloud height, which contributed to the near solar–infrared compensation at lower latitudes, is in effect offset by reduced insolation at higher latitudes, such that again the model predicts near compensation for the changes in absorbed solar and outgoing infrared radiation.

However, Manabe and Wetherald (1980) emphasize: "In view of the uncertainty in the values of the optical cloud parameters and the crudeness of the cloud prediction scheme incorporated into the model, it is premature to conclude that the change of cloud cover has little effect on the sensitivity of climate." The potential importance of cloud feedback effects has been emphasized by a number of Australian scientists (e.g., Pearman, 1980). There have also been suggestions (e.g., Petukhov *et al.*, 1975; Charlock, 1981; Hunt, 1981; Wang *et al.*, 1981) that changes in cloud optical properties associated with climatic change might be important in modeling cloudiness–radiation feedback. Thus, the suggestion of solar–infrared compensation is at best tenuous; and even if this were to be the case on a global scale, there may be important regional exceptions. Moreover, if small changes in cloud amount are important, they will be difficult to predict from model calculations.

Alternative approaches toward estimating the relative solar–infrared components of cloudiness–radiation feedback involve empirical studies using Earth radiation budget data. In one such approach, Cess (1976) has suggested solar–infrared compensation, whereas Ohring and Clapp (1980) and Hartmann and Short (1980) have suggested that the solar component dominates over

Principal Scientific Issues in Modeling Studies

the infrared component by roughly a factor of 2. Cess employed the satellite data compilation of Ellis and Vonder Haar (1976), while the other two studies utilized radiation budget data derived from NOAA scanning radiometer measurements. Recently, Cess *et al.* (1982) have reviewed these studies and suggest that the conclusions of solar dominance might be attributable to the NOAA data's being derived from narrow spectral measurements.

Clearly, the empirical approaches comprise an important means of studying the cloudiness–radiation feedback problem. The approach by Ohring and Clapp (1980) is particularly attractive. They have employed interannual variability in regional monthly-mean radiation data, from which they estimate the relative solar–infrared cloudiness feedback components by attributing this variability to interannual variability in cloudiness. We recommend re-examination of their conclusions employing radiation budget data that do not suffer the possible deficiencies noted above.

In summary, while it is conceivable that cloudiness–radiation feedback does not substantially influence climate sensitivity, it is clear that additional studies of this feedback mechanism are necessary. This will be a difficult problem that will require a multifaceted approach. One should not trust model prediction schemes until they produce meaningful simulations of observed seasonal cloud cover and the seasonal radiation components. At present, there are no published models that do this. While the empirical approach offers an attractive means of attacking the problem, it will require clarification of sampling bias within Earth radiation budget data.

Stratus–Sea-Ice Interactions

In simple climate models, ice–snow albedo feedback contributes substantially to the CO_2 warming at high latitudes. However, it seems likely that in regions where sea ice is reduced, evaporation will increase and possibly lead to increased low-level stratus cloud cover, which would reflect solar radiation and at least partially reduce the albedo feedback. This effect is not certain to occur, because altered atmospheric temperature profiles due to added CO_2 could also cause a decrease of cloud cover. Examination of 3-D GCM experiments with doubled CO_2 (Manabe and Wetherald, 1980; Hansen *et al.*, 1982) show an increase of cloud cover of several percent in the region where the added CO_2 melts the sea ice. The change of planetary albedo is 4 times smaller than the change of ground albedo, as a result of both cloud shielding of the ground and increased local cloud cover with increased CO_2. This result must be considered tentative, in view of the great oversimplification of the calculation of clouds in climate models, but it serves to emphasize the possible importance of cloud processes.

TABLE 2.2 Equilibrium Global-Mean Surface-Temperature Effect of Indicated Changes in Abundance of Several Trace Gases as Computed Using an RC Model (Lacis et al., 1981)

Gas	Hypothetical Abundance Change	Temperature Change (°C)
CO_2	300 ppm → 600 ppm	2.9
N_2O	0.28 ppm → 0.56 ppm	0.6
CH_4	1.6 ppm → 3.2 ppm	0.3
$CCl_2F_2 + CCl_3F$	0 → 2 ppb each	0.6
O_3	25% decrease	−0.5

TRACE GASES OTHER THAN CO_2

Most modeling endeavors concerning the CO_2–climate problem address only the question of the climatic response to increasing atmospheric CO_2, while the amounts of other atmospheric gases remain fixed. But associated changes, either climatologically or anthropogenically induced, of minor atmospheric constituents can also be of significance. For example, Ramanathan (1975) suggested that chlorofluoromethane (CFM) concentrations of only a few parts per billion (ppb) could produce a significant global warming. Subsequently, Wang et al. (1976) analyzed the climatic response to changes in a number of atmospheric trace gases.

Trace atmospheric gases that absorb in the infrared may enhance or counteract CO_2 warming if their abundance should change (Ramanathan, 1975; Wang et al., 1976). In general, if these gases increase, they will lead to warming, although for gases that are inhomogeneously mixed, such as ozone (O_3), the temperature change could be in either direction depending on changes in the vertical distribution of the gas. A comparison of the equilibrium global-mean surface-temperature effect of changes in several trace gases is shown in Table 2.2, based on calculations with a model having a sensitivity of 2.8°C for doubled CO_2 (Hansen et al., 1981). While this table illustrates the importance of trace gases, there is a considerable difference between this calculation and other model results for CFM's. The model results of Ramanathan (1975), Reck and Fry (1978), and Karol (1981) show a global surface warming of 0.8–0.9 K for CFM increase from 0 to 2 ppb.

There are several ways in which the amount of a climatologically important atmospheric trace gas might be altered—for example,

• As a consequence of the direct anthropogenic emission of the gas into the atmosphere, as is the case for CFM's;
• As a result of the anthropogenic emission of gas or gases that, through interactive atmospheric chemistry, alter the amounts of climatologically

Principal Scientific Issues in Modeling Studies

important trace gases (e.g., increasing anthropogenic emissions of CO are expected to increase the amounts of tropospheric CH_4 and O_3 (Rowland and Molina, 1975; Logan et al., 1978; Hameed et al., 1980), both of which are greenhouse gases (see Table 2.2));

• Owing to biospheric changes caused by CO_2 warming, e.g., increased CH_4 production by warmer wetland areas or the release of CH_4 now trapped as a hydrate in permafrost regions;

• Owing to altered atmospheric temperature and water-vapor concentration resulting from increased atmospheric CO_2, which would produce changes in atmospheric chemistry and therefore in trace-gas abundances.

We begin by discussing the last of the above items. While an increase in atmospheric CO_2 would warm the surface and troposphere, the stratosphere would be likely to cool as a consequence of enhanced CO_2 emissions. This raises the possibility of a change in stratospheric ozone as a consequence of temperature-dependent stratospheric chemistry. However, model studies (Luther et al., 1977; Boughner, 1978) show that for doubled CO_2 the column density of O_3 would be increased by only 1–3 percent, which would produce an insignificant climate feedback. A second possible interaction pertains to the troposphere. CO_2-induced tropospheric warming would produce increased tropospheric water vapor, which, from a radiation standpoint, would result in the well-known positive climate feedback. But as a consequence of tropospheric chemistry, the increased H_2O would reduce tropospheric CH_4 and O_3. Since CH_4 and O_3 are both greenhouse gases, this aspect of the process comprises a negative climate feedback. Employing coupled climate–chemical models, both of which are vertically averaged 1-D (latitude) models, Hameed et al. (1980) have found that the global warming produced by a 70 percent increase in atmospheric CO_2 would result in 15 and 10 percent reductions, respectively, in tropospheric CH_4 and O_3. The resulting negative feedback would, however, be quite minor, reducing the CO_2-induced global warming by about 10 percent.

Such decreases in tropospheric CH_4 and O_3 do not account for increasing anthropogenic emissions of CO, CH_4, and NO_x resulting from the fossil-fuel burning that produced the increased atmospheric CO_2. Logan et al. (1978) and Hameed et al. (1980) have suggested that such anthropogenic emissions could lead to significant increases in tropospheric CH_4 and O_3 during the next century, with a corresponding enhancement of the CO_2-induced global warming. In the latter study, the CH_4 and O_3 increases were obtained despite the previously discussed negative chemical feedback due to tropospheric water vapor. It should be emphasized that, although the troposphere contains only 10 percent of the total O_3, the infrared opacity of tropospheric O_3 is,

TABLE 2.3 Scenario for Global Trace-Gas Alterations (from Ramanathan, 1980)

| Period | Mixing Ratios by Volume ||||% O_3 Change||
	CO_2 (ppm)	CH_4 (ppm)	N_2O (ppm)	CFM's (ppb)	Tropo-sphere	Total
Pre-1940	300	1.4	0.3	0	0	0
22nd century	600	3.3	0.6	2.2	100	−6.5

because of enhanced pressure broadening, nearly the same as that of stratospheric O_3 (Ramanathan and Dickinson, 1979). Predictions of O_3 and CH_4 changes, based on biogeochemical cycles, are of course very uncertain.

Other human activities such as the growing use of nitrogen fertilizers could lead to increases in atmospheric concentrations of N_2O and CFM's. As illustrated in Table 2.2, both are significant greenhouse gases. Moreover, CFM's, through interactive stratospheric chemistry, may additionally lead to a reduction in stratospheric O_3 (Logan et al., 1978). Recently, Ramanathan (1980) assumed a steady-state scenario for alterations in trace gases from their assumed values prior to 1940, and their subsequent climatic impacts, that incorporates the consequences of fossil-fuel burning as well as anthropogenic emissions of CFM's and N_2O. The hypothetical increase in trace gases is assumed to occur in the same time period for which a doubling of CO_2 occurs. This scenario was compiled from a variety of sources, including carbon-cycle models, photochemical models, and future energy-consumption models; it is summarized in Table 2.3. Although tropospheric O_3 is assumed to double, the total ozone amount decreases because of increasing CFM's, which reduce stratospheric O_3. This also results in a change in the vertical distribution of stratospheric O_3. Thus, although the radiative effects of trace gases are almost additive, their influences can be chemically coupled.

The climatic effects of the trace-gas alterations shown in Table 2.3 are quite substantial. The twofold CO_2 increase produces, with Ramanathan's RC model,* a global warming of 2.0°C, but when the other trace-gas changes are included, global warming is increased to 3.6°C. Put another way, the model scenario suggests that roughly 40 percent of the global warming would be due to changes in trace gases other than CO_2. While the model scenario is of course highly uncertain, it nevertheless serves to illustrate the possible climatic importance of anthropogenic changes of trace gases.

---

*Note that this model has fixed cloud altitude and is thus less sensitive by about 40–60 percent than the model used to generate the 2 × CO_2 value in Table 2.2 that fixes cloud temperature.

Principal Scientific Issues in Modeling Studies

To date, the only known significant change in trace-gas abundance (other than that of CO_2) has been in the CFM's, which have increased from an essentially zero abundance a few decades ago to 0.3 ppb of CCl_2F_2 and 0.2 ppb of CCl_3F (Mendonca, 1979), for which the equivalent greenhouse warming is roughly 0.06°C. No major trend of O_3 abundance (either tropospheric or stratospheric) has been observed. N_2O has been monitored for several years, and small but significant increases have recently been detected (Weiss, 1981). Although there have been tentative suggestions of a slight increase in CH_4 over the past decade (Hudson and Reed, 1979; Heidt and Ehhalt, 1980; Graedel and McRae, 1980; Rasmussen and Khali, 1981), this gas has not been carefully monitored. But atmospheric chemical models (Logan et al., 1978; Hameed et al., 1980) indicate that the CH_4 abundance may be very sensitive to anthropogenic influences, and it is therefore recommended that careful monitoring of CH_4 be initiated.

Our knowledge of the atmospheric concentrations of these radiatively active trace constituents before the mid-nineteenth century is quite poor. Information is potentially available from tree rings, corals, and glacial ice, and some estimates of CO_2 concentrations have been made (e.g., Berner et al., 1980). Better knowledge of past concentrations of these gases would greatly facilitate direct assessment of their effects on global climate.

In summary, the estimated net impact of measured changes of trace gases during this century has been an estimated equilibrium warming of 0.1–0.2°C, which is substantially smaller than the estimated equilibrium warming of roughly 0.5°C for the estimated increase of 45 ppm of CO_2 during the same period, both numbers being based on a model with 2.8°C sensitivity for doubled CO_2. However, since model studies indicate that trace-gas abundances might change significantly in the future, it is important to monitor the primary trace gases, because they could significantly enhance future CO_2 warming.

ATMOSPHERIC AEROSOLS

In addition to changes in atmospheric CO_2 and other trace gases, atmospheric aerosols provide another potentially significant source of climate variability. But this problem is far more complex than that involving trace-gas changes, since the radiation effects of the aerosols depend on their composition, size, and vertical and global distributions. Stratospheric aerosols, which persist for a few years following major volcanic eruptions, can produce a substantial reduction in global surface temperature and can explain much of the observed natural climatic variability (Hansen et al., 1981; Gilliland, 1982). Such an aerosol is composed primarily of aqueous sulfuric acid droplets (Rosen, 1971), and its main climatic impact is to backscatter solar radiation, thus reducing the amount of solar radiation that is absorbed by the Earth–atmosphere system. There is a partially modifying heating due to the infrared greenhouse effect of the aerosols (Pollack *et al.*, 1976), but the net aerosol effect is surface cooling. Although there are indications of an anthropogenic source of stratospheric aerosols (Hofmann and Rosen, 1980), it is not clear if or when this will become significant in comparison with volcanic sources.

The climatic effect of tropospheric aerosols is much less certain. Although anthropogenic aerosols are noticeable in regions near their sources, there does not appear to have been a significant long-term increase in the aerosol level in remote regions of the globe except possibly in the Arctic, where substantial concentrations of anthropogenic aerosols build up during the winter and spring (Roosen *et al.*, 1973; Cobb, 1973; Rahn and McCaffrey, 1980; Shaw, 1981). However, no long-term trend in this anthropogenic aerosol has yet been established. The natural aerosol consists of sulfates, marine aerosols, and windblown dust. Both sulfates and windblown dust could increase as the result of man's activities, the former owing to industrial activity (Bolin and Charlson, 1976) and the latter owing to agricultural activities and desertification. Increased tropospheric sulfates would lead to global cooling. With respect to windblown dust, recent measurements indicate a midsolar imaginary refractive index (which governs absorption) of roughly 0.01 (Patterson *et al.*, 1977; Carlson and Caverly, 1977; and Patterson, 1981), and aerosol–climate models that employ this value (Ohring, 1979; Coakley *et al.*, 1982) suggest that increased windblown dust would also lead to cooling on a *global* scale, but perhaps with important regional exceptions. Because this aerosol absorbs a significant amount of solar radiation, it could lead to an albedo decrease over highly reflecting regions such as deserts and to an albedo increase over darker regions such as oceans (Coakley *et al.*, 1982).

An additional anthropogenic component of tropospheric aerosols is industrial soot, which, because it is highly absorbing, would lead to global warming (e.g., Hansen *et al.*, 1981). Again, however, it must be emphasized that insufficient observations have been made to determine global trends for this aerosol component. But recent chemical and optical analyses of Arctic haze indicate that during the spring and early summer the haze particles contain a high concentration of graphite carbon (Porch and MacCracken, 1981, based on work by Rosen), and it has been suggested that this Arctic soot may be influencing the Arctic climate (Budiansky, 1980). Recently, Porch and MacCracken (1982) have modeled the possible effects of carbonaceous aerosols on the Arctic climate, and they found that the springtime Arctic soot could lead to an average heating rate of 0.06 K day^{-1} in the lowest 5 km of the atmosphere under cloud-free conditions. Interestingly enough, this is similar to estimated heating rates at northern latitudes that are due to a doubling of atmospheric CO_2.

In summary, variations in stratospheric aerosols have continued and will continue to be dependent on volcanic activity, contributing to natural climatic variability. Although there is currently no evidence that a global trend exists in the components of tropospheric aerosols, future anthropogenic changes in tropospheric aerosols are possible. But the climatic impact of such changes, if indeed they occur, cannot currently be determined. Because of the differing optical properties of the individual components of tropospheric aerosols, one cannot even conclude that possible future anthropogenic changes in aerosol loading would produce global heating or global cooling. Furthermore, increased tropospheric aerosols could influence cloud optical properties (Charlock and Sellers, 1980) and thus possibly modify cloudiness–radiation feedback as discussed in the section Cloudiness–Radiation Feedback.

VALIDATION OF CLIMATE MODELS

Need for Model Validation

Mathematical-physical models, whether in a highly simplified form or as an elaborate formulation of the behavior and interaction of the global atmosphere, ocean, cryosphere, and biomass, are generally considered to be the most powerful tools yet devised for the study of climate. This is in part due to the reproducibility (and in this sense the objectivity) of a model's results, in part to the opportunity to trace cause-and-effect relationships within a consistent framework of interacting processes, and in part to the possibility of performing numerical experiments under a wide variety of conditions. Our confidence in climate models comes from a combination of tests of the correctness of the models' parameterizations of individual processes and comparisons of the models' sensitivity to observed seasonal variations. All models, however, require the parameterization of a number of subgrid-scale processes important to climate, such as cloudiness, precipitation, and the radiative and turbulent heat fluxes in the planetary boundary layer. The more realistic climate models also simulate the transient synoptic-scale eddies of middle and higher latitudes and therefore display an inherent variability or noise in their climatic statistics.

Each of the above factors influences the extent to which we can (or should) trust the results of climate models, and all are aspects of the general validation problem. While the absolute accuracy of a model may be of greatest interest to the scientist, a knowledge of the uncertainty of a model's results may be of equal or greater importance to those using or acting on the results. This is especially true in the case of the CO_2–climate problem, in which decisions of immense economic and social consequences may be made on the basis of information supplied by models. The validation of climate models is therefore becoming an increasingly important matter and should be undertaken on a systematic and sustained basis; a comprehensive validation program would include the assembly of a wide variety of observational data specifically for the purpose of model validation and the development of a validation methodology.

The validation of numerical climate models comes from a hierarchy of tests at different levels, many of which are part of the stock in trade and are normally not published. Detection of outright errors in a complex computer code is a formidable task that requires extraordinary care. Tests are also made to see if the behavior in isolation of individual subsystems, such as the boundary layer or the treatment of radiation, resembles that established from field or laboratory observations or from more detailed models based on known physical principles. The parameters used in a well-constructed climate model are mostly explicitly derived from such comparisons and are not subject to arbitrary adjustment or tuning.

Every investigator establishes in a more or less systematic manner the sensitivity of the conclusions to the boundary conditions applied (such as the distribution of continents and oceans) and to the parameterizations used. Only the more significant sensitivities are singled out for explicit discussion in the literature, but accepted models are based on the judgments of many individuals independently exploring approaches that are similar in kind but different in detail. An important role is played by highly simplified models that approximately reproduce the behavior of the more elaborate models; such models can be used to explore rapidly a wide variety of situations and to identify key experiments for more elaborate investigation. Only with such a background of testing for internal consistency and reasonable overall structure and behavior does the comparison of model output with actual observational data begin.

Present State of Model Validation

The primary method for validating a climate model is to determine how well the model-simulated climate compares with observations. Usually some verification against observed data is performed during the preliminary testing of a model, especially in those models with a large number of parameterized processes, and here it is important to distinguish between model calibration or tuning and model validation. When, for example, the local heat capacity in an energy-balance climate model is adjusted to give a realistic phase and amplitude for the seasonal variation of surface temperature, then this temperature variation can no longer be used to verify the model's performance. However, the solutions (if any) for other processes and variables predicted by the model could be used for validation, as could variations of the temperature, provided they were not on the same scales of space and time

Principal Scientific Issues in Modeling Studies

used to calibrate the model in the first place. In some models the imposition of particularly influential boundary conditions is also a form of model calibration, in that variables closely associated with the prescribed conditions cannot be used for independent model validation. An example is the surface-air temperature simulated over the oceans in a GCM in which the sea-surface temperature has been prescribed.

Most climate models have been given at least preliminary validation in terms of a comparison of climatological averages with the simulated time means of selected climatic variables. In the case of GCM's, for example, such validation has usually included the sea-level pressure, the temperature and geopotential at one or more levels in the free air, and the total precipitation as simulated for a month or season in comparison with the corresponding climatological distributions. In terms of these and other variables, modern climate models provide a reasonably satisfactory simulation of the large-scale global climate and its average seasonal changes. Even here, however, the different sets of observed data that have been used for validation are not of the same quality, and the effects of uneven data coverage are not taken into account. For many of the variables simulated in a climate model it is difficult to find suitable observational data sets available for model validation, even though these variables may be ones in which there is great practical interest (see the section Detection Strategies). Examples of such data are the cloudiness, the surface evaporation and heat flux, and the soil moisture, commonly simulated in GCM's, and the parameterized fluxes of heat and moisture, commonly simulated in one- and two-dimensional models.

As important as the time-averaged distributions of the climatic variables themselves may be, the simulated variance, covariance, and other higher-order statistics are of equal importance in the validation of a climate model. Only a limited amount of such verification has been made for GCM's because of the need for extended integrations and the lack of the needed observational statistics. Many of the more highly parameterized models, moreover, address at most only an equilibrium seasonal climate and thus do not simulate either the seasonal or the interannual variability associated with the transient synoptic-scale eddies. The validation of the equilibrium statistics of such models is therefore confined to the comparison of equilibrium fields with long-term seasonal climatology.

In addition to verification in terms of time-averaged statistics, an important aspect of climate-model validation is the confirmation of the essential correctness of the major physical parameterizations in the model. Chief among these are the model's treatment of clouds and their effects on radiation, the variations of snowcover and sea ice, and the surface exchanges of heat and moisture; in no climate model do these parameterizations rest on completely satisfactory theoretical or empirical bases. If climate models are to project future climate changes correctly in response, say, to increased levels of atmospheric CO_2, then their parameterizations must be valid under as wide a range of conditions as possible (i.e., they should work for the right reasons). In contrast to the extended global integrations required for the validation of a climate model's overall performance, the validation of the parameterization of specific physical processes can often be accomplished with specialized observations in a local region for a limited period of time. Such "process" validation is the aim of several large-scale observational programs either now under way or in the planning stages.

The behavior of climate models is also influenced to some extent by the treatment of land-surface processes such as albedo and evapotranspiration. These depend on vegetation coverage and may interact with climate change in ways that are as yet poorly understood. This interaction is particularly significant for regional processes such as desertification, deforestation, and the distribution of precipitation.

It is recognized that a major uncertainty about predictions of CO_2-induced climate change is due to the fact that the atmospheric models have not been coupled to realistic ocean models. In this connection, an important technical issue is to devise computationally efficient schemes to couple climatic subsystems with order-of-magnitude different response times (e.g., the atmosphere and oceanic mixed layer). Asynchronous coupling has been used in this connection, but such schemes can distort the transient behavior of coupled atmosphere–ocean models (e.g., Dickinson, 1981; Ramanathan, 1981). In order to maximize the number of numerical experiments performed within a fixed computing budget, it is important to investigate the errors inherent in various asynchronous coupling schemes.

There is also skepticism that any model calibrated to today's climate will be useful for predicting a future climate in which both the ocean and atmosphere could be much different. In the case of the ocean, there is nothing equivalent to the historical data set based on daily global observations that is available for the atmosphere. This view overlooks new sources of data that are now available or will soon become available for testing water-mass models of the ocean. In addition to the traditional hydrographic data for the global ocean, which provide the fields of time-averaged temperature and salinity, satellites and ship-of-opportunity data have now provided rough maps of mesoscale eddy intensity. In addition, the GEOSECS program and the follow-up Transient Tracers Program have provided two invaluable 3-D synoptic pictures of the penetration of tritium into the northern hemisphere oceans since its injection during the weapons tests of the 1960's. Data on other tracers such as bomb-produced ^{14}C and radon are not so extensive but still provide valuable constraints for models. While the existing data base represents an inadequate sampling of the large-scale density structure over many parts of the world ocean, ocean models are beginning to reach a level of development where these data can be used for verification (Haney, 1979; Huang, 1979; Bryan and Lewis, 1979). Recently, the mesoscale statistics of the North Atlantic have been predicted in a high-resolution model (Holland and Rhines, 1980).

For ocean models used in the study of the transient response of climate, anthropogenic tracers such as tritium and bomb-produced ^{14}C are particularly valuable. These tracers show how particles introduced at the surface are carried downward. The data set collected by the GEOSECS program and cooperating groups provides a useful verification for ocean transport models.

In view of the importance of the ocean in the response of climate to increasing CO_2, it is recognized that the development of ocean models to a level comparable with that of atmospheric models is a matter of urgency. It is recommended that the requirements of ocean models be given high priority in the planning of oceanographic field programs planned by the World Climate Research Program.

Much has been learned with atmospheric models without an ocean component. In the same way, much can be learned with an ocean model coupled to a very simple atmospheric model or one with specified boundary conditions. There are many complex problems in developing coupled ocean–atmosphere models, not the least of which is that the atmospheric models have been calibrated without active oceans. There is no need, however, to wait until fully tested, universally accepted coupled models are available before moving beyond the oversimplified 1-D models now being used to interpret the tracer data and estimate transient climate response.

An inadequate but growing body of data exists for verifying models of ice-pack formation and movement. Satellites provide data on the extent of the ice, and satellite-tracked beacons are providing a new data set on the movement of ice. Less adequate is the information on ice-thickness distribution in the polar oceans. Models of the ice pack designed for climate-response calculations have been verified against the observed distribution of ice (Parkinson and Washington, 1979; Parkinson and Kellogg, 1979; Hibler, 1981), but the level of verification in a fully integrated climate model is less satisfactory (Manabe and Stouffer, 1980).

Planetary Studies

One useful test of the greenhouse theory can be obtained from empirical examination of other planets that in effect provide an ensemble of experiments over a wide range of conditions. The atmosphere of Mars, when it is dust-free, is relatively transparent in the infrared, and the greenhouse effect is hardly measurable. However, frequent dusty conditions and the small

TABLE 2.4 Greenhouse Effect on Terrestrial Planets[a]

Planet	Observed or Estimated					T_e (K)	T_s (K)		
	S_0 (W m^{-2})	A	τ_e	Γ (°C km^{-1})	H (km)		Eq. (1)	Eq. (2)	Observed
Mars	589	0.15	~0.1	5	1	217	221	222	~220
Earth	1367	0.30	~1	5.5	6	255	293	288	288
Venus	2613	0.75	~100	7	70	232	685	720	~700

[a]S_0 solar irradiance; A, planetary albedo; τ_e, effective infrared optical thickness; Γ, mean lapse rate between surface and mean radiating level; H, altitude of mean radiating level; T_e, effective radiating temperature; and T_s, surface air temperature. Equation (1) is the radiative approximation of greenhouse effect, $T_s = T_e (1 + 3/4\tau_e)^{1/4}$, whereas Equation (2) is the convective approximation $T_s = T_e + \Gamma H$.

magnitude of horizontal energy transport by the atmosphere permit study of the greenhouse mechanism on a local basis (Gierasch and Goody, 1972).

On Earth, water vapor and clouds make the troposphere too opaque for pure radiative transfer of heat with a stable lapse rate. The mean lapse rate is $\Gamma \sim 5-6°C$ km^{-1}, which is less than the dry adiabatic value ($\sim 10°C$ km^{-1}) because of latent heat release by condensation as moist air rises and cools and because the atmospheric motions that transport heat vertically include large-scale atmospheric dynamics as well as local convection. The mean radiating level occurs in the midtroposphere, at altitude $H \sim 6$ km. The atmosphere of Venus is opaque to infrared radiation for most altitudes between the surface and the cloudtops, owing to CO_2, H_2O, and aerosol absorption. The lapse rate is near the dry adiabatic value for the predominantly CO_2 atmosphere ($\sim 7°C$ km^{-1}), because of the absence of large latent heat effects and the small effect of large-scale dynamics on the vertical temperature gradient. The cloudtops radiating to space are at altitude $H \sim 70$ km.

Observed surface temperatures of Mars, Earth, and Venus (Table 2.4) confirm the existence, nature, and magnitude of the greenhouse effect. Climatological data being collected by spacecraft at Venus and Mars will permit more precise analyses of radiative and dynamical mechanisms that affect the greenhouse warming. Of course, these planetary tests do not validate the current predictions for CO_2 warming on Earth, but they do help provide confidence in the predicted magnitude of the equilibrium greenhouse warming due to a given atmospheric composition. The planets also provide the potential for greater tests of 3-D atmospheric models: it should ultimately be possible to use basically the same model for different planets, changing parameters such as solar constant, planet's gravity, rate of rotation, atmospheric density, and composition and in this way obtain a better understanding of basic mechanisms.

Alternative Modeling Approaches

Laboratory experiments on the behavior of differentially heated rotating fluids have provided insight into a number of basic hydrodynamic processes that are relevant to the circulation of the atmosphere and ocean. For example, the structure of such features as jet streams (Fultz *et al.*, 1959; Dolzhanskiy and Golitsyn, 1977; Hide, 1977; Pfeffer *et al.*, 1980) and the dynamics of baroclinic instablility have been examined under a wide range of geophysically relevant conditions. Laboratory experiments can also contribute to our understanding of certain other processes such as small-scale turbulence and mixing. However, laboratory models cannot simulate usefully the majority of the climatically important physical processes such as the effects of changes in radiatively active gases, aerosols, albedo, and other surface characteristics and the hydrologic cycle and cloudiness. Nevertheless, laboratory modeling studies (and their numerical counterparts) may be useful for study of the dynamic conditions that may occur in a CO_2-enriched climate. They should be interpreted insofar as possible in terms of the processes that need to be properly parameterized in large-scale circulation models.

Improvement of Model Validation

In order to improve our knowledge of the performance of climate models and to increase their ability to project the climate changes likely to result from increased atmospheric CO_2 in particular, we recommend that a climate-model validation methodology be developed and that it be vigorously pursued for as many documented models as possible.

As key elements of such a validation methodology, we recommend:

• The systematic determination of the statistical properties of the performance of a hierarchy of climate models, including the geographical and seasonal distribution of the simulated means and higher-order statistics of modeled variables and processes. This evaluation should include a statement of the uncertainty or error bars of all climatic statistics, as determined from control integrations of appropriate length.

• The systematic assembly of a standardized climatological data base for model validation, with the statistics of all available climatic variables, processes, and boundary conditions determined on time and space scales consistent with those resolved in climate models. Those elements of such a validation data base that now exist should be identified and efforts made to tap effectively all current observational programs of climatic relevance.

• The development of appropriate regional or local observational data sets for the purpose of validating specific climate-model parameterizations, such as stratiform and convective cloudiness, the radiative effects of aerosols, and the subgrid scale fluxes of heat and moisture over both the ocean and vegetated land.

• The design and adoption of a set of universal sensitivity tests under standardized conditions, in which the performance of all climate models would be systematically compared with each other as well as with the model's performance under normal or control conditions. Such experiments might include, for example, changes in the solar constant (say, ± 2 percent), the surface albedo (say, ± 10 percent), and of course changes in the atmospheric CO_2 concentration (say, a doubling and a quadrupling). After such intercalibration, standardized transient response experiments with time-dependent climate models would provide useful further validation. In these, for example, a step-function increase of atmospheric CO_2 could be prescribed and the response calculated over 50 years.

• The development of diagnostic and statistical techniques that would provide greater insight than do present methods into the physical and dynamical processes responsible for a modeled change of climate. Of particular value would be techniques to permit the attribution or "tagging" of climatic changes as due to increased CO_2 rather than to other factors. We also recommend that climate-model performance be evaluated in terms of phenomenological measures and information as needed in climate-impact assessment, such as number of rainy days, storm tracks, frosts, drought, degree days, growing season, and extreme temperatures.

• The systematic assembly of climate information from paleoclimates and other sources such as planetary atmospheres, which are helpful in the validation of climate models.

3
Predictions and Scenarios of Climate Changes Due to CO_2 Increases

DEVELOPMENT OF PREDICTIONS AND SCENARIOS

A primary objective of climate-model development and related research is to improve the ability to make predictions of the response of the climate system to some internal or external change, such as increases in atmospheric CO_2 concentrations. These predictions explicitly or implicitly consist of estimates of the probability of future climatic conditions due to the altered parameters or inputs and unavoidably entail uncertainties arising from model inadequacies, errors in input data, inherent indeterminacy in the climate system, and other sources. The extent of uncertainties may vary greatly with the detail of the prediction, so that, for example, regional predictions may be more uncertain than global-average predictions, and monthly predictions more uncertain than annual ones.

The utility of a particular prediction depends on both the detail and the uncertainty associated with the prediction and on the use to which the prediction is put. A reliable prediction that increasing CO_2 may produce global warming may be misleading to a person concerned with a particular locality if it is not accompanied by some estimate of the regional distribution of the global warming; some regions, for example, may experience no warming, a cooling, or even some combination of these depending on season or year. Similarly, reliable predictions of hydrologic changes may be needed in order to assess correctly the likely impacts of a warming on crops or on water supply.

Nevertheless, internally consistent and detailed specifications of climatic conditions over space and time may be extremely useful for analysis of social

Predictions and Scenarios of Climate Changes

responses and sensitivities to climatic changes. In this report, we term such specifications "scenarios." While scenarios are naturally chosen to exclude conditions believed to be impossible, it is important to recognize that they are research tools—*substitutes* for predictions—not forecasts, to which objectively quantifiable degrees of credence may be attached. Assignment of relative priorities to members of a group of scenarios would, of course, constitute a probabilistic prediction.

Climate models provide the opportunity to generate both predictions and scenarios of climate changes due to increasing CO_2. As discussed extensively in the previous chapter, a carefully validated model should, within the bounds of the model and the validation procedure, be able to reproduce realistically the basic characteristics of the present climate or other observed climates. If the basic processes that control climate are reasonably well taken into account in the model, it should then be possible to simulate the behavior of the climate for a range of inputs and parameters. Thus, as discussed in the following section, numerical experiments with a variety of climate models have been performed that yield information on how the climate system might behave in response to a CO_2 increase, e.g., a doubling. In the case of global-average and perhaps zonal-average estimates of temperature changes associated with a given increase in CO_2, climate models appear realistic enough to provide estimates of some reliability. However, for more detailed geography and for parameters other than temperature (e.g., windiness, soil moisture, cloudiness, and solar insolation), present climate models are not sufficiently realistic to give reliable estimates. Nevertheless, these models can still suggest scenarios of how the climate might change and provide a basis for further integration of both model and observational results.

Observational studies of both present and past climates are important for both predictions and scenarios of climate changes. First, these studies can be used to check the reliability of climate models for a variety of different conditions; if a particular model is able to reproduce the characteristics of several different climates that are known to have existed, one has greater confidence that the model takes into account all relevant processes. Second, if a climate model exhibits large climatic changes due to some perturbation such as a CO_2 increase, observational studies can demonstrate directly or by analogy that such large changes are indeed possible. For example, by confirming the existence of an ice-free Arctic Ocean in past epochs, paleoclimatic studies have lent some credence to model predictions of vanishing ice for greatly increased CO_2. Finally, observational studies can help corroborate and fill out model-generated scenarios of climatic changes. They can, for example, suggest relationships between global or regional changes and local phenomena, between model-simulated parameters such as temperature and other potentially important parameters such as windiness and soil moisture, and between equilibrium and transient responses of the climate system as a whole or its components. These uses of observational studies are discussed more extensively in the section Observational Studies of Contemporary and Past Climates.

MODEL STUDIES

Numerical Experiments with Climate Models

Mathematical models of climate with a wide range of complexity have been used to estimate climate changes resulting from an increase in CO_2 concentration in the atmosphere. These models include not only 1-D RC models but also comprehensive GCM's of the joint ocean–atmosphere system.

Two kinds of numerical experiments have been conducted by use of climate models. An experiment of the first kind may be called a "CO_2 transient response experiment," which seeks to investigate the temporal variation of climate caused by a continuous increase of CO_2 concentration in the atmosphere. Starting from an equilibrium climate of a model with a normal CO_2 concentration, a climate model is time-integrated with a prescribed CO_2 concentration as a function of time.

One of the key factors that control the transient response of the model climate is the thermal inertia of the oceans. Unfortunately, GCM's of the joint ocean–atmosphere system are still in an early stage of development. A few studies of CO_2 transient response experiments have begun to appear in the literature and are the subject of discussion in the section Role of the Oceans.

An experiment of the second kind may be called a "CO_2–climate equilibrium sensitivity experiment." It evaluates the total equilibrium response of the climate to a given increase of CO_2 concentration by examining the difference between a model climate with normal CO_2 concentration and another model climate with an above-normal concentration.

In the following subsections, predictions of CO_2-induced climate changes based on the results from the several numerical experiments of the second kind, i.e., CO_2-climate sensitivity experiments, are reviewed.

Global-Average Response

Temperature. On the basis of comparative assessment of the results from the wide varieties of climate models, the Charney report estimated the equilibrium global surface warming resulting from the doubling of CO_2 concentration to

Predictions and Scenarios of Climate Changes 51

be "near 3°C with a probable error of ± 1.5°C."* *The present panel has not found any new results that necessitate substantial revision of this conclusion.*

Table 3.1 contains predicted area-mean increases of surface air temperature obtained from various recent experiments with GCM's of climate. The range of these results for a doubling of CO_2 (i.e., about 2–4°C) falls within the uncertainty indicated in the Charney report. (For discussion of the results from simplified models of climate, see the section Global Climate Sensitivity—Simplified Models and Empirical Approaches.) An extensive discussion of the differences among these estimates of warming was included in the Charney report and is not repeated here. (See also World Meteorological Organization, 1979a, 1979b.) One should point out, however, that the estimates by Gates *et al.* (1981) and Mitchell (1979) included in Table 3.1 for completeness are much smaller than the others because the imposed condition of fixed sea-surface temperature places a strong constraint on the changes of surface air temperatures in their model atmospheres.

In contrast to the warming of the troposphere, both RC models and GCM's indicate that a cooling of the stratosphere would result from an increase of CO_2 concentration in the atmosphere. The enhanced emission from the stratosphere upward into space and downward into the troposphere is responsible for this cooling. In general, the magnitude of this stratospheric cooling would be much larger than that of the tropospheric warming and would have a relatively small latitudinal variation. According to the latest study by Fels *et al.* (1980), the predicted cooling due to the doubling of CO_2 concentration with other stratospheric conditions fixed is about 7°C and 11°C at altitudes of 30 and 45 km, respectively.

Hydrology. Sensitivity studies with GCM's suggest that the global-mean rates of both evaporation and precipitation would increase with higher atmospheric CO_2 concentrations. The physical mechanism for the intensification of the hydrologic cycle was discussed, for example, by Manabe *et al.* (1965), Manabe and Wetherald (1975), Wetherald and Manabe (1975), and Schneider *et al.* (1978). It should be noted here that this does not necessarily imply an overall increase (or reduction) in the soil wetness. Table 3.2 presents the results of several sensitivity studies and shows the percentage difference in the intensity of the models' hydrologic cycles between normal CO_2 concentrations and two levels of above-normal CO_2 concentrations. This, together with the results presented in Table 3.1, indicates that a model with a larger

---

*Our understanding is that the Charney group meant this to imply a 50 percent probability that the true value would lie within the stated range.

TABLE 3.1 Estimates from Numerical Model Experiments of the Warming of Area-Mean Surface Air Temperature $\overline{\Delta T}^A$ (°C) Resulting from Doubling of CO_2 Concentration in the Atmosphere

Reference	Geography	SST[a]	Insolation	Cloud	$\overline{\Delta T}^A$ (°C) Doubling
Interactive Ocean					
Manabe and Wetherald (1975)	Idealized	Predicted	Annual	Prescribed	2.9
Manabe and Wetherald (1980)	Idealized	Predicted	Annual	Predicted	3.0
Wetherald and Manabe (1981)	Idealized	Predicted	Annual	Prescribed	3.0[b]
Wetherald and Manabe (1981)	Idealized	Predicted	Seasonal	Prescribed	2.4[b]
Manabe and Stouffer (1979, 1980)	Realistic	Predicted	Seasonal	Prescribed	2.0[b]
Hansen et al. (1979)	Realistic	Predicted	Annual	Predicted	3.9
Hansen et al. (1979)	Realistic	Predicted	Seasonal	Predicted	3.5
Schlesinger (1982)	Realistic	Predicted	Seasonal	Predicted	2.0
Noninteractive Ocean					
Gates et al. (1981)	Realistic	Prescribed	Seasonal	Predicted	0.3
Mitchell (1979)	Realistic	Prescribed	Seasonal	Prescribed	0.2

[a]Sea-surface temperature.
[b]Temperature changes inferred from the results of numerical experiments in which the atmospheric CO_2 concentration is increased by a factor of 4.

Predictions and Scenarios of Climate Changes

TABLE 3.2 Percentage Increase of Area-Mean Rates of Precipitation (or Evaporation) Resulting from Doubling (or Quadrupling) of CO_2 Concentration in a Model Atmosphere

Reference	Doubling (%)	Quadrupling (%)
Idealized Geography		
Manabe and Wetherald (1975)[a]	7	
Manabe and Wetherald (1980)[a]	7	12
Wetherald and Manabe (1981)[a]		13
Wetherald and Manabe (1981)		10
Realistic Geography		
Manabe and Stouffer (1979, 1980)		7
Hansen et al. (1979)[a]	6	
Hansen et al. (1979)	4	

[a]No seasonal variation of insolation.

CO_2-induced warming tends to have a larger increase in the overall intensity of the hydrologic cycle. It therefore appears probable that the doubling of CO_2 concentrations would result in the overall intensification of the hydrologic cycle by several percent.

Zonal-Average Response

Temperature. Climate sensitivity studies indicate that the CO_2-induced increase of surface air temperature would have significant latitudinal and seasonal variations. For example, the predicted annual-mean warming of surface air in the polar regions is 2–3 times as great as the corresponding warming in the tropical region. The surface air warming over the Arctic Ocean would be significantly greater than the corresponding warming over the Antarctic continent, where the effect of the snow-albedo feedback mechanism is relatively small. In low latitudes, the increase of surface air temperature would be relatively small because moist convection would distribute the CO_2 heating over the entire depth of the troposphere.

The sensitivity studies of Manabe and Stouffer (1979, 1980) also indicate that a CO_2-induced increase of surface air temperature would have a large seasonal variation over the Arctic Ocean and the surrounding regions (see Figure 3.1). This Arctic warming would be at a minimum in summer and at a maximum in winter as influenced by sea ice. In low latitudes, the amplitude of seasonal variation would be small.

Hydrology. The study of the hydrologic changes induced by an increase of the atmospheric CO_2 concentration has just begun, and it is not yet possible

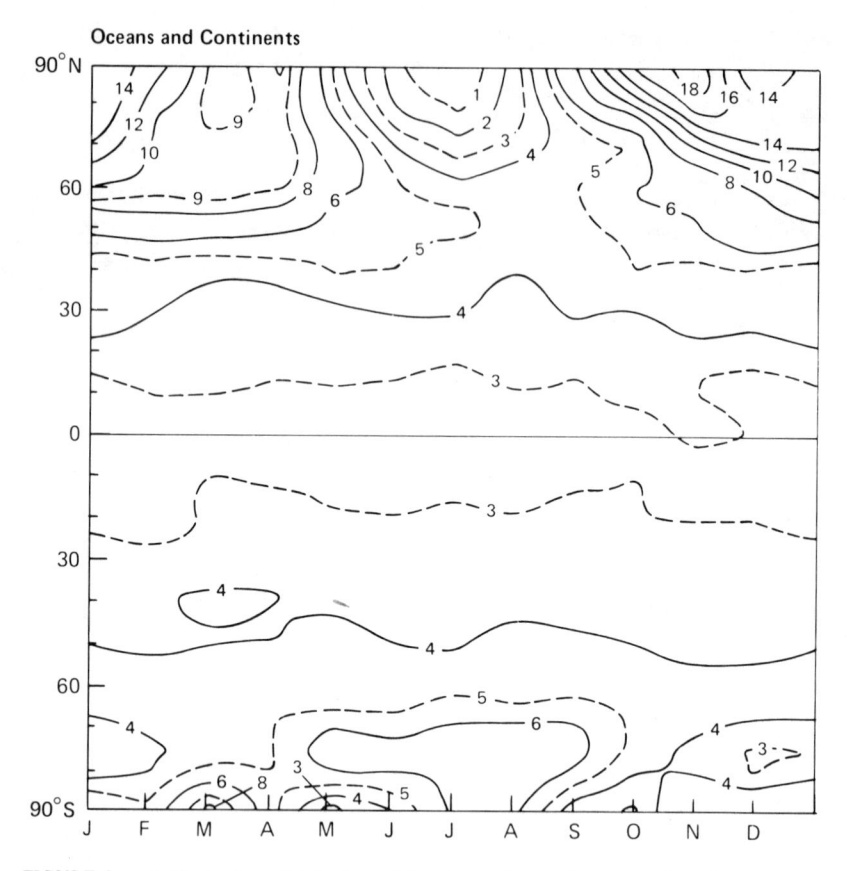

FIGURE 3.1 Latitude–time distribution of the change in zonal-mean surface air temperature (°C) resulting from quadrupling atmospheric CO_2 concentration (Manabe and Stouffer, 1979, 1980).

to make reliable predictions of the latitudinal distributions of hydrologic changes. Unlike the temperature response to a CO_2 doubling, the soil moisture response is of the same order of magnitude as the climatological interannual variability, and thus a lower signal-to-noise ratio is obtained in these experiments. However, some statistically significant zonal-mean hydrologic changes have been consistently identified in a number of numerical sensitivity experiments (Manabe and Stouffer, 1980; Wetherald and Manabe, 1981; Manabe et al., 1981). These zonal-mean results are listed below for future evaluation. The uncertainties in these results do not permit more than qualitative statements.

1. The zonally averaged annual mean rate of runoff of the models increases markedly over polar and surrounding regions, where precipitation increases substantially owing to the penetration of moisture-rich, warm air into high latitudes (i.e., poleward of 60° N).

2. In the zonal mean, the models' snowmelt season with large runoff rate arrives earlier because of the large warming of surface air in high latitudes (i.e., north of 60° N), and the model's snowfall begins later.

3. During summer, the northern hemisphere zonal-mean value of soil moisture in the models decreases in middle and high latitudes (i.e., north of 35° N). The earlier ending of the spring snowmelt season mentioned above implies the earlier beginning of the period of relatively large evaporation rates and, accordingly, less soil moisture during summer in higher latitudes (i.e., poleward of 30° N). In addition, another factor contributes to the summer dryness in middle latitudes. The reduction in the rainfall rate between spring and summer occurs earlier because of the earlier beginning of the summer period of low storminess, resulting in a reduction of soil moisture.

4. The zonal-mean area coverage and thickness of sea ice over the Arctic and circum-Antarctic oceans in the models decrease in response to an increase of atmospheric CO_2 concentration.

Geographical Distribution of Climate Changes

Local climate has a much larger temporal variability than the zonal-mean or global-mean climate. In order to distinguish a CO_2-induced climate change from the natural variations in the local model climate, an extensive time integration of a climate model is required. The results from such studies are not available at present. Furthermore, the geographical distribution of hydrologic variables (i.e., precipitation rate) as simulated by current climate models contains many unrealistic features. Because of these problems, reliable predictions of the geographical distribution of the CO_2-induced climate change are not now possible.

Future efforts should be directed toward the further improvement of the parameterizations of physical processes that are poorly understood at present (i.e., cloud formation, moist convection, and land-surface processes). In view of the poor performance of current climate models in simulating the distribution of precipitation in the neighborhood of major mountain ranges, the dynamical computation of the flow field over and around mountains requires improvement. To determine the geographical details of a CO_2-induced climate change, it would also be necessary to develop a climate model with improved computational resolution.

OBSERVATIONAL STUDIES OF CONTEMPORARY AND PAST CLIMATES

Use of Observational Studies

Observational studies play an important role in three areas: (1) the formulation of ideas and models of how climate operates, (2) the general validation of theories and models, and (3) the construction of climate scenarios. Both contemporary (e.g., this century) and past climatic data sets are useful in all three areas. The role of contemporary data sets in these three areas is well known and requires no elaboration. The role of past climatic data sets is perhaps less generally recognized. An example of the use of past climatic data is provided by the work of CLIMAP Project Members (1976) in developing a set of observations of the climate at the time of the last glacial maximum around 18,000 years before present. In a narrow sense, the charts of ocean-surface temperature, sea ice, land albedo, and ice-sheet topography can be viewed as a climate scenario for a glacial world. However, these observations along with related studies of the time-dependent behavior of climate before and after glacial maximum (Hays *et al.*, 1976; Ruddiman and McIntyre, 1979) have also led to significant advances in climate theory, and the data sets have also been useful for climate-model validation (Gates, 1976).

The CO_2 sensitivity studies with climate models have indicated that CO_2-induced climatic changes might become large in comparison with recent natural climatic fluctuations. Because the changes may be large, the relative importance of observational studies of past climatic data is increased. That is, the short period of instrumental climate records has been characterized by relatively small variations in climate, none of which match the magnitude of the ultimate change that might result from a doubling of the atmospheric CO_2 concentrations. Only the past climate records can provide material for observational studies of atmosphere, ocean, cryosphere, and biosphere variations of the magnitude suggested by the CO_2 sensitivity studies.

The status of these observational studies is briefly reviewed in the following subsections.

Contemporary Climatic Data

The results of the Global Weather Experiment are now being analyzed and will provide a unique data base for model calibration and validation studies of one seasonal cycle (Joint Organizing Committee, 1979). Recent progress in defining the specific characteristics of certain interannual variations (in particular, the Southern Oscillation) are providing an opportunity for climate modeling experiments, for validations of short-term climatic variations, and for improved understanding of the physics of climate.

Predictions and Scenarios of Climate Changes

An exciting development in climate theory has been the quantification of the role of volcanic eruptions in producing short-term climatic changes (e.g., Mass and Schneider, 1977; Hansen *et al.*, 1981; Gilliland, 1982). The interpretation of the climatic response to volcanic eruptions involves such matters as the treatment of radiative effects of aerosols and the delayed response of climate produced by the large thermal inertia of the oceans. This work provides some validation for models as one begins to treat the different set of somewhat analogous problems related to CO_2 increase.

Several studies have attempted to composite individual "warm" years (or seasons) for the purpose of searching for "warm-earth" climatic patterns (Namias, 1980; Wigley *et al.*, 1980; Williams, 1980; Pittock, 1980). While these studies have been useful, they have certain problems and limitations that deserve comment:

1. The climatic variations of individual years (or seasons) are presumably due to factors other than slow changes in the CO_2 concentration.
2. The composites consist of extreme "years," whereas extreme "decades" might provide more useful indicators of changes in the slow-responding parts of the climate system.
3. Even the composites based on extreme years do not produce global- or zonal-average climatic differences (composite minus long-term mean) that approach in magnitude the corresponding CO_2-induced climatic changes that have been simulated in CO_2-sensitivity studies.
4. The emphasis so far has been on studies of atmospheric parameters (such as precipitation and surface air temperature); other variables of the ocean and cryosphere need more attention.
5. The emphasis has been on observational studies of "warm" periods rather than "warming" periods; the latter are important for identifying the transient response.
6. Most of the observational studies use the CO_2 sensitivity study simulations of large temperature increases in polar latitudes as a basis for choosing candidates for composites; if theory or models suggest other regions or variables that might be sensitive to CO_2 changes, then alternative composites should be studied.

To summarize this subsection, the various observational studies (only a few of which have been mentioned) have provided a useful starting point for diagnosis of climatic processes that may prove to be relevant to the CO_2 problem. There are, as noted above, certain inherent weaknesses to the approach, and more attention should be given to these problems. The currently available results do not provide a firm basis for climatic assessment of possible CO_2-induced climatic changes, nor should they be considered adequate at present for validation of CO_2 sensitivity studies with climate models.

Past Climatic Data

There is mounting evidence that the varying distribution of solar radiation associated with orbital variations (Hays et al., 1976) is an important factor in climatic change on the 10^4–10^5-year time scale. Observational studies of past climate can document these changes so that any response to changes in solar radiation forcing from model calculations can be compared with observations. These studies are aiding in the development of a theory of large-scale climatic changes in response to external changes in solar radiations.

A possibly important feature of past climates is revealed by the recent work by Berner et al. (1980) and Delmas et al. (1980), which points to large changes in CO_2 concentration over the past 20,000 years (more CO_2 about 5000 years ago and less before 10,000 years ago). Even if these CO_2 changes did not initiate climatic change, they may amplify the change and could provide extremely useful knowledge about large-scale feedback processes that operate at the glacial–interglacial scale of climate variations, a point made recently by Thompson and Schneider (1981).

Several individuals and groups are beginning to examine past climatic data for the purpose of developing "warm-earth" climate reconstructions (Kellogg, 1977; Butzer, 1980; Pittock, 1980). A sequence of workshops (Kellogg and Schneider, 1981) has been proposed that would bring together a multidisciplinary group to work on this problem area. Although there are few published papers in this area at this time, it is possible to address some of the same problems, limitations, and opportunities that apply to contemporary climatic data sets.

1. Past climate data sets can probably be identified that have the same magnitude of change as that predicted for CO_2-induced climatic change. The period 5000–7000 years ago, or perhaps a previous interglacial, may be such a period, but further work will be necessary to confirm, reject, or modify this conjecture. Much effort will be required to calibrate the past climate sensors (fossil plankton, pollen, geomorphic features, for example) in quantitative terms for comparison with climate-model simulations.

2. As with contemporary data sets, past climate data sets provide the potential for observing many components of the climate system: ocean, land surface, cryosphere. Moreover, such paleoclimatic reconstructions can provide a great deal of insight into regional climate changes on a warmer Earth and notable distributions of temperature, rainfall, and soil moisture of major importance for biological productivity. However, the assembly of past climate

data sets is a major multidisciplinary effort (CLIMAP, 1976; Peterson et al., 1979). Careful dating control is essential, and this is a serious limitation of many past climate data sets at present.

3. As with contemporary data studies, there has been an emphasis on "warm" periods rather than "warming" periods. The best opportunity for studies of transients on the order of decadal time scales is probably confined to the last several thousand years, when tree-ring data, laminated lake or ocean sediment data, and laminated ice-core data provide accurate time control.

4. As with contemporary studies, it is desirable that studies should consider a variety of past climates; a narrow focus on only one or two candidate reconstructions is probably too restrictive in view of current knowledge—in terms of both knowing what to look for (i.e., model predictions) and what to expect (i.e., current knowledge about a specific interval of the past climatic record).

Various possibilities have been suggested:

(a) Comparisons of the hypsithermal climate (5000–7000 years ago) with present climate. Evidence indicates that this was the interglacial maximum and that it was warmer then than now, at least in selected locations.

(b) Comparisons of the last glacial maximum (about 18,000 years ago) with the present climate. It was colder (global-average surface temperature was about 5°C colder than it is at present; Gates, 1976; Manabe and Hahn, 1977; Peterson et al., 1979), and it was a time of maximum ice volume.

(c) Studies of various times between glacial maximum, interglacial maximum, and present conditions, coupled with information on the changing patterns of solar radiation (from orbital parameter changes) and possible changes of CO_2 concentration, provide the potential for rather detailed study of the process of large climatic changes that involve the ocean and cryosphere in a major way.

(d) Studies of the previous interglacial maximum (around 120,000 years ago). Sea-level evidence suggests that it might have been warmer than the current interglacial.

(e) Studies of the late Tertiary period (about 3×10^6 to 12×10^6 years ago), when there was an ice-free Arctic Ocean.

We recommend that interdisciplinary workshops be held to assess these possibilities (and others) and organize the work.

To summarize, the past climate studies are not so advanced as the studies with contemporary data sets. This is not surprising in view of the large multidisciplinary effort that will be required to acquire the data and carry out the analysis. Nevertheless, the past climatic studies are potentially very valuable because they deal with large changes of the climate system, including the oceans and the cryosphere, because they can reveal regional patterns of climate change, and because there is knowledge of the changes in forcing that are driving the system (solar radiation and perhaps some CO_2-feedback effects).

As with contemporary studies, the currently available reconstructions based on past climatic data are useful starting points for further work but are not yet adequate for model validation studies or impact studies.

4
Development of Monitoring and Early Detection Strategies

CURRENT STATUS

Attempts have been made to detect an atmospheric warming caused by the past increase of CO_2 concentrations in the atmosphere (Madden and Ramanathan, 1980; Hansen et al., 1981; Kukla and Gavin, 1981; Wigley and Jones, 1981). However, such a warming has not been unequivocally identified, perhaps for the following reasons:

1. As discussed in the section Role of the Oceans, the full manifestation of the CO_2-induced warming may be delayed because of the large thermal inertia of oceans.
2. The CO_2-induced warming may be masked by climate changes caused by other factors such as the secular variations of atmospheric aerosols and solar irradiance.
3. Since the records from instrumented observations of the past climate variation are available over a relatively short period, it is difficult to obtain a long enough record of the natural variability of climate to establish the statistical significance of a CO_2-induced signal.

DETECTION STRATEGIES

It has been suggested that the long-term variation of global-mean (or hemispheric-mean) atmospheric temperature has been influenced by the changes in insolation and atmospheric aerosol concentrations (e.g., Budyko, 1969; Hoyt, 1979; Hansen et al., 1981; Gilliland, 1982). Climate variations due to these non-CO_2 influences must be quantified to the extent possible in order to permit the climate changes attributable to CO_2 to be identified. It is therefore advisable to monitor the temporal variations of atmospheric aerosol concentration and spectra of solar and terrestrial radiation at the top of the atmosphere and at the Earth's surface. In addition, it is desirable to monitor the concentrations of some minor atmospheric constituents, such as fluorocarbons, methane, and nitrous oxide, that may contribute to future changes of the atmospheric temperature as discussed in the section Trace Gases Other Than CO_2. Other candidates for monitoring include planetary albedo as influenced by deforestation and desertification. On the basis of these measurements, one should be able to distinguish the climate changes attributable to changes in these factors and thereby facilitate the detection of a CO_2-induced climate signal. A comprehensive set of variables should be monitored in order to discriminate CO_2-induced changes from changes in climate caused by other factors. These variables should include CO_2 concentration in the atmosphere, the solar irradiance, the spectral distribution of solar and terrestrial radiation (at the top and bottom of the atmosphere), and concentrations of aerosol and minor constituents in the atmosphere. Other variables derivable from existing records and observing programs may provide indications of CO_2 effects. These include total precipitable water and the diurnal range or temperature.

For the earliest detection of a CO_2-induced climate signal, it is desirable to monitor a set of variables that reveals CO_2-induced changes at the earliest possible time. Preliminary attempts to identify such indicators have already been made by Madden and Ramanathan (1980) and Wigley and Jones (1981). For example, these studies noted that the zonal-mean surface air temperatures in summer, except at very high latitudes, have relatively large signal-to-noise ratios. Also, zonal-mean summer temperatures in the stratosphere and mesosphere are expected to show large CO_2-induced cooling, whereas the natural temperature variability is relatively small. However, since the radiation balance of these regions is largely independent of the troposphere, observations of stratospheric and mesospheric cooling would only confirm that CO_2 concentrations had increased and that an approximately correct radiation model had been used. Moreover, changes in other constituents, e.g., ozone, could confuse the signal. The effects of changing CO_2 concentrations on atmospheric radiation transfer may also be monitored by looking for systematic trends in satellite remote temperature sounding data, which depend on infrared radiance from atmospheric CO_2. Another possible candidate for consideration is the temperature of deep ocean layers (see the section Monitoring Ocean Climate Response).

One of the meteorological variables that are useful for monitoring the past and future climate change is the global-mean (or hemispheric-mean) surface air temperature of the atmosphere. This variable has been used in some attempts to detect the CO_2 climatic signal partly because it has a large signal-to-noise ratio. It is expected that the CO_2-induced temperature change is positive in most of the troposphere, whereas the natural temperature variation changes sign from one geographical location to another. Therefore, the signal-to-noise ratio for an area-mean temperature should increase as the area for the averaging increases.

One can also introduce indices that are better suited for the early detection of CO_2-induced climate change. One example of such an index is the weighted mean global (or hemispheric) mass integral of the atmospheric temperature. The weighting factor may be defined such that it is small in the regions of large natural temperature fluctuation and large in the regions where the CO_2-induced temperature change is expected to be large from model experiments. Obviously, one can devise many other similar indices. A set of indices that have a large signal-to-noise ratio should be identified and monitored.

From the preceding discussion, it is clear that the early detection of the CO_2–climate signal requires not only a prediction of the CO_2-induced climate change but also a knowledge of the natural climate variabilities. Therefore, it is necessary to determine (from the past climatic records) the variability of relevant climatic variables such as temperatures of the atmosphere and oceans. For example, some of the important variables requiring improved determination are hemispheric- and global-mean surface air temperatures. The present information on the temporal variation of these quantities may contain inaccuracies of a substantial magnitude (Damon and Kunen, 1976, 1978; Carter, 1978; Barnett, 1978). Emphasis should be placed on the compilation and analysis of past climate data to acquire more reliable reconstructions of past variations of climate on a variety of space scales. Finally, it should be noted that a major workshop convened by the Department of Energy in June 1981 addressed the problem of early detection. Its report was not available in time for the panel's consideration, but it will clearly shed much light on the problem.

MONITORING OCEAN CLIMATE RESPONSE

Operational monitoring of the ocean's response to climate change requires observation of sea-surface temperature, water-mass parameters, and sea-ice extent. The problem with sea-surface temperature measurements is their large fluctuations due to mesoscale eddies and observational errors. However, changes in the heat content of the ocean may possibly be detectable over periods of a decade or longer.

Water-column observations have the potential of being able to monitor directly the temperature and salt response of the ocean for a range of isopycnals, all with differing time responses. Of particular importance to this monitoring will be the wind-driven gyres, which have a decadal time scale (Jenkins, 1980). The monitoring of potential temperature and salinity changes on isopycnals in the wind-driven gyres may provide an early indication of climatic change. The gradients of potential temperature and salinity along isopycnals are weak in the wind-mixed gyres; the only signature of the mesoscale eddy field would be that of small fluctuations along isopycnals. These measurements thus have an inherently large signal-to-noise ratio.

Estimates based on a series of four cruises in the eastern North Atlantic subtropical gyre show that potential temperature can be spatially determined in the presence of eddies to an error less than 0.02°C for any cruise and a scatter less than 0.1°C for four cruises extending over 2 years.

The difficulty in interpreting any water-mass indicators of climatic variability is that poorly understood salinity changes associated with evaporation and precipitation may accompany these changes. It is unlikely, however, that temperature and salinity changes should coincide to produce no apparent change on any isopycnal. Measurements of varying quality and geographical distribution exist that date back to the 1920's.

The extent of sea ice has been shown by Manabe and Stouffer (1980) to respond sensitively to CO_2-induced climatic changes in models. Paleoclimatic reconstructions of sea-ice extent in the southern hemisphere by Hays (1978) and correlations between northern hemisphere ice extent and surface temperatures (e.g., Vinnikov and Groisman, 1981; Vinnikov et al., 1980) seem to indicate a strong direct relationship between them. Indeed, reductions in sea-ice extent in both hemispheres have recently been noted from satellite observations (Kukla and Gavin, 1981). Since sea-ice extent is easily and routinely measured from satellites, it should be a good parameter for monitoring CO_2-induced climatic changes.

References

Aagaard, K., L. K. Coachman, and E. Carmak (1981). On the halocline of the Arctic Ocean, *Deep Sea Res. 28A*, 529–545.

Arrhenius, S. (1896). On the influence of carbonic acid in the air upon the temperature of the ground, *Philos. Mag. 41*, 237.

Bach, W., J. Pankrath, and J. Williams (1980). *Interactions of Energy and Climate*, D. Reidel, Boston, Massachusetts.

Barnett, T. P. (1978). Estimating variability of surface air temperature in the northern hemisphere, *Mon. Weather Rev. 106*, 1353.

Berner, W., H. Oeschger, and B. Stauffer (1980). Information on the CO_2 cycle from ice core studies, *Radiocarbon 22*, 227.

Bolin, B. (1981). Changing global biochemistry, Rep. CM-52, Dept. of Meteorol., U. of Stockholm, 24 pp.

Bolin, B., and R. J. Charlson (1976). On the role of the tropospheric sulfur cycle in the shortwave radiative climate of the Earth, *Ambio 5*, 47.

Bolin, B., E. T. Degens, S. Kempe, and P. Ketner, eds. (1979). *The Global Carbon Cycle*, SCOPE 13, Proceedings of a SCOPE Workshop, Ratzeburg, German Federal Republic, March 21–26, 1977, John Wiley and Sons, New York, 491 pp.

Boughner, R. E. (1978). The effect of increased carbon dioxide concentrations on stratospheric ozone, *J. Geophys. Res. 83*, 1326.

Bryan, K., and L. J. Lewis (1979). A water mass model of the World Ocean, *J. Geophys. Res. 84*, 2503.

Budiansky, S. (1980). New attention for atmospheric carbon, *Environ. Sci. Technol. 14*, 1430.

Budyko, M. I. (1969). The effect of solar radiation variations on the climate of the Earth, *Tellus 21*, 611.

Butzer, K. W. (1980). Adaptation to global environmental change, *Prof. Geog. 32*, 269.

Callendar, G. S. (1938). The artificial production of carbon dioxide and its influence on temperature, *Q. J. R. Meteorol. Soc. 64*, 223.

Carlson, T. N., and R. S. Caverly. (1977). Radiative characteristics of Saharan dust at solar wavelengths, *J. Geophys. Res. 82*, 3141.

Carter, J. R. (1978). Letter concerning the paper "Global Cooling?" *Clim. Change 1*, 383.

Cess, R. D. (1976). Climate change: an appraisal of atmospheric feedback mechanisms employing zonal climatology, *J. Atmos. Sci. 33*, 1831.

Cess, R. D. (1978). Biosphere-albedo feedback and climate modeling, *J. Atmos. Sci. 35*, 1765.

Cess, R. D., B. P. Briegleb, and M. S. Lian (1982). Low-latitude cloudiness and climate feedback: comparative estimates from satellite data, *J. Atmos. Sci.* (in press).

Chamberlin, T. C. (1899). An attempt to frame a working hypothesis of the cause of glacial periods on an atmospheric basis, *J. Geol. 7*, 545.

Charlock, T. P. (1981). Cloud optics as a possible stabilizing factor in climate change, *J. Atmos. Sci. 38*, 661.

Charlock, T. P., and W. D. Sellers (1980). Aerosol, cloud reflectivities and climate, *J. Atmos. Sci. 31*, 1136.

CLIMAP Project Members (1976). The surface of the ice-age Earth, *Science 191*, 1131.

Climate Research Board (1979). *Carbon Dioxide and Climate: A Scientific Assessment*, National Academy of Sciences, Washington, D.C., 22 pp.

Climate Research Board (1980). Letter Report of the Ad Hoc Study Panel on Economic and Social Aspects of Carbon Dioxide Increase, National Academy of Sciences, Washington, D.C., 11 pp.

Coakley, J. A., R. D. Cess, and F. B. Yurevich (1982). The effect of aerosols upon the Earth's radiation budget: a parameterization for application to climate models, *J. Atmos. Sci.* (submitted).

Cobb, W. E. (1973). Oceanic aerosol level deduced from measurements of the electrical conductivity of the atmosphere, *J. Atmos. Sci. 30*, 101.

Damon, P. E., and S. M. Kunen (1976). Global cooling? *Science 193*, 447.

Damon, P. E., and S. M. Kunen (1978). Reply to Letter Concerning the Paper "Global Cooling?", *Climatic Change 1*, 387.

Delmas, R. J., J.-M. Ascencio, and M. Legrand (1980). Polar ice evidence that atmospheric CO_2 20,000 yr BP was 50% of present, *Nature 284*, 155.

Dickinson, R. E. (1980). Convergence rate and stability of ocean-atmosphere coupling schemes with a zero-dimensional climate model, *J. Atmos. Sci. 38*, 2112–2120.

Dolzhanskiy, F. V., and G. S. Golitsyn (1977). Laboratory modeling of global geophysical flows (a review), *Izv. Atmos. Oceanic Phys. 13*, 550.

Ellis, J. S., and T. H. Vonder Haar (1976). Zonal average earth radiation budget measurements from satellites for climate studies, Atmos. Sci. Paper 240, Colorado State U., Fort Collins, Colorado, 50 pp.

Fels, S. B., J. D. Mahlman, M. D. Schwarzkopf, and R. W. Sinclair (1980). Stratospheric sensitivity to perturbations in ozone and carbon dioxide: radiative and dynamical response, *J. Atmos. Sci. 37*, 2265.

Fine, R. A., J. L. Reid, and H. G. Ostlund (1981). Circulation of tritium in the Pacific Ocean, *J. Phys. Oceanog. 11*, 3.

Fultz, D., R. R. Long, G. V. Owens, W. Bohan, R. Kaylor, and J. Weil (1959). *Studies of Thermal Convection in a Rotating Cylinder with Some Implications for Large-Scale Atmospheric Motions*. Meteorological Monographs 4, No. 21, American Meteorological Society, Boston, Massachusetts, 104 pp.

Gates, W. L. (1976). The numerical simulation of ice-age climate with a global general circulation model, *J. Atmos. Sci. 33*, 1844.

Gates, W. L., K. H. Cook, and M. E. Schlesinger (1981). Preliminary analysis of experiments on the climatic effects of increased CO_2 with an atmospheric general circulation model and a climatological ocean model, *J. Geophys. Res. 86*, 6385.

Geophysics Study Committee (1977). *Energy and Climate*, National Academy of Sciences, Washington, D.C., 158 pp.

References

Gierasch, P. J., and R. M. Goody (1972). The effect of dust on the temperature of the Martian atmosphere, *J. Atmos. Sci. 29*, 400.

Gilliland, R. L. (1982). Solar, volcanic and CO_2 forcing of recent climate change, *Clim. Change 4* (in press).

Graedel, T. E., and J. F. McRae (1980). On the possible increase of the atmospheric methane and carbon monoxide concentrations during the last decade, *Geophys. Res. Lett. 7*, 977.

Hameed, S., R. D. Cess, and J. S. Hogan (1980). Response of the global climate to changes in atmospheric chemical composition due to fossil fuel burning, *J. Geophys. Res. 85*, 7537.

Haney, R. L. (1979). Numerical models of ocean circulation and climate interaction, *Rev. Geophys. Space Phys. 17*, 1494.

Hansen, J. E., W.-C. Wang, and A. A. Lacis (1978). Mt. Agung eruption provides test of a global climatic perturbation, *Science 199*, 1065.

Hansen, J. E., et al. (1979). *Proposal for Research in Global Carbon Dioxide Source/Sink Budget and Climate Effects*, Goddard Institute for Space Studies, New York, 60 pp.

Hansen, J., D. Johnson, A. Lacis, S. Lebedeff, P. Lee, D. Rind, and G. Russell (1981). Climate impact of increasing atmospheric carbon dioxide, *Science 213*, 957.

Hansen, J., A. Lacis, D. Rind, G. Russell, and P. Stone (1982). (in preparation).

Hartmann, D. L., and D. A. Short (1980). On the use of earth radiation budget statistics for studies of cloud and climate, *J. Atmos. Sci. 37*, 1233.

Hays, J. D. (1978). A review of the late quaternary climatic history of Antarctic seas, in *Antarctic Glacial History and World Paleoenvironments*, E. M. Van Zindern Bakker, ed., A. A. Balkema, Rotterdam, The Netherlands, pp. 57-71.

Hays, J. D., J. Imbrie, and N. J. Shackleton (1976). Variations in the Earth's orbit: pacemaker of the ice ages, *Science 194*, 1121.

Heidt, L. E., and D. H. Ehhalt (1980). Corrections of methane concentrations measured prior to 1974, *Geophys. Res. Lett. 7*, 1023.

Hibler, W. D., III (1980). Modeling a variable thickness sea ice cover, *Mon. Weather Rev. 108*, 1943.

Hide, R. (1977). Experiments with rotating fluids, *Q. J. R. Meteorol. Soc. 103*, 1-28.

Hoffert, M. I., A. J. Callegari, and C.-T. Hsieh (1980). The role of deep sea heat storage in the secular response to climatic forcing, *J. Geophys. Res. 85*, 6667.

Hofmann, D. F., and J. M. Rosen (1980). Stratospheric sulfuric acid aerosol layer: evidence for an anthropogenic component, *Science 208*, 1368.

Holland, W. R., and P. B. Rhines (1980). An example of eddy-induced oceanic circulation, *J. Phys. Oceanog. 10*, 1010.

Hoyt, D. V. (1979). An empirical determination of the heating of the Earth by the carbon dioxide greenhouse effect, *Nature 282*, 388.

Huang, J. C. K. (1979). Numerical case studies for oceanic thermal anomalies with a dynamic model, *J. Geophys. Res. 84*, 5717.

Hudson, R. D., and E. I. Reed (1979). *The Stratosphere: Present and Future*, NASA Ref. Publ. 1049, 432 pp.

Hunt, B. G. (1981). An examination of some feedback mechanisms in the carbon dioxide climate problem, *Tellus 33*, 78.

Idso, S. B. (1980a). The climatological significance of a doubling of Earth's atmospheric carbon dioxide concentration, *Science 207*, 1462.

Idso, S. B. (1980b). Carbon dioxide and climate (reply to Schneider et al., 1980, and Leovy, 1980), *Science 210*, 7.

Idso, S. B. (1981). Carbon dioxide: an alternative view, *New Sci. 92*, 444.

JASON (1979). *The Long Term Impact of Atmospheric Carbon Dioxide on Climate*, Tech. Rep. JSR-78-07, SRI International, Arlington, Virginia, 184 pp.

JASON (1980). *The Carbon Dioxide Problem: DOE Program and a General Assessment*, Tech. Rep. JSR-80-06, SRI International, Arlington, Virginia, 39 pp.

Jenkins, W. J. (1980). Tritium and ³He in the Sargasso Sea, *J. Mar. Res. 38*, 533.

Joint Organizing Committee (1975). *The Physical Basis of Climate and Climate Modelling*, GARP Publ. Ser. No. 16, Joint Planning Staff, Global Atmospheric Research Programme, Geneva, Switzerland, 265 pp.

Joint Organizing Committee (1979). *Report of the JOC Study Conference on Climate Models: Performance, Intercomparison and Sensitivity Studies*, Vols. I and II, GARP Publ. Ser. No. 22, W. L. Gates, ed., Joint Planning Staff, Global Atmospheric Research Programme, Geneva, Switzerland, 1049 pp.

Kandel, R. S. (1981). Surface temperature sensitivity to increased atmospheric CO_2, *Nature 293*, 634.

Kaplan, L. D. (1960). The influence of carbon dioxide variations on the atmospheric heat balance, *Tellus 12*, 204.

Karol, I. (1981). *Report of the US/USSR Workshop on Carbon Dioxide and Climate*, Leningrad, June 15–20.

Kellogg, W. W. (1977). *Effects of Human Activities on Global Climate*, Tech. Note No. 156, World Meteorological Organization No. 486, Geneva, Switzerland, 47 pp.

Kellogg, W. W., and S. H. Schneider (1981). Proposal to the Department of Energy, Washington, D.C., for partial support of the Preliminary Workshop on CO_2-Induced Climate Scenarios (1981) and the Second Workshop on CO_2-Induced Climate Scenarios (1982), National Center for Atmospheric Research, Boulder, Colorado, 6 pp.

Kukla, G., and J. Gavin (1981). Summer ice and carbon dioxide, *Science 214*, 497–503.

Lacis, A., J. Hansen, P. Lee, T. Mitchell, and S. Lebedeff (1981). Greenhouse effect of trace gases, 1970–1980, *Geophys. Res. Lett. 8*, 1035–1038.

Lindzen, R. S., A. Y. Hou, and B. F. Farrell (1982). The role of convective model choice in calculating the climate impact of doubling CO_2, *J. Atmos. Sci.* (in press).

Logan, J. A., M. J. Prather, S. C. Wofsy, and M. B. McElroy (1978). Atmospheric chemistry: response to human influence, *Trans. R. Soc. 290*, 187.

Luther, F. M., D. J. Wuebbles, and J. S. Chang (1977). Temperature feedback in a stratospheric model, *J. Geophys. Res. 82*, 4935.

Madden, R. A., and V. Ramanathan (1980). Detecting climate change due to increasing carbon dioxide, *Science 209*, 763.

Manabe, S., and D. G. Hahn (1977). Simulation of the tropical climate of an ice age, *J. Geophys. Res. 82*, 3889.

Manabe, S., and R. J. Stouffer (1979). A CO_2-climate sensitivity study with a mathematical model of the global climate, *Nature 282*, 491.

Manabe, S., and R. J. Stouffer (1980). Sensitivity of a global climate model to an increase of CO_2 concentration in the atmosphere, *J. Geophys. Res. 85*, 5529.

Manabe, S., and R. T. Wetherald (1967). Thermal equilibrium of the atmosphere with a given distribution of relative humidity, *J. Atmos. Sci. 24*, 241.

Manabe, S., and R. T. Wetherald (1975). The effects of doubling the CO_2 concentration on the climate of a general circulation model, *J. Atmos. Sci. 32*, 3.

Manabe, S., and R. T. Wetherald (1980). On the distribution of climate change resulting from an increase in CO_2 content of the atmosphere, *J. Atmos. Sci. 37*, 99.

Manabe, S., J. Smagorinsky, and R. F. Strickler (1965). Simulated climatology of a general circulation model with a hydrologic cycle, *Mon. Weather Rev. 93*, 769.

Manabe, S., R. T. Wetherald, and R. J. Stouffer (1981). Summer dryness due to an increase of atmospheric CO_2 concentration, *Clim. Change 3*, 347.

References

Mass, C., and S. H. Schneider (1977). Statistical evidence on the influence of sunspots and volcanic dust on long-term temperature records, *J. Atmos. Sci. 34*, 1995.

Mendonca, B. G. (1979). *Geophysical Monitoring for Climatic Change 7*, Environmental Research Laboratory, National Oceanic and Atmospheric Administration, Boulder, Colorado.

Mitchell, J. F. B. (1979). Preliminary report on the numerical study of the effect on climate of increasing atmospheric carbon dioxide, Met.O.20, Tech. Note No. II/137, Meteorological Office, Bracknell, Berks., U.K., 12 pp.

Möller, F. (1963). On the influence of changes in the CO_2 concentration in air on the radiation balance of the Earth's surface and on the climate, *J. Geophys. Res. 68*, 3877.

Munk, W. H. (1966). Abyssal recipes, *Deep Sea Res. 13*, 707.

Namias, J. (1980). Some concomitant regional anomalies associated with hemispherically averaged temperature variations, *J. Geophys. Res. 85*, 1585.

Newell, R. E., and T. G. Dopplick (1979). Questions concerning the possible influence of anthropogenic CO_2 on atmospheric temperature, *J. Appl. Meteorol. 18*, 822.

Newell, R. E., and T. G. Dopplick (1981). Reply to Robert G. Watts' Discussion of "Questions Concerning the Possible Influence of Anthropogenic CO_2 on Atmospheric Temperature," *J. Appl. Meteorol. 20*, 114.

NOAA (1980). *National Climate Program Five-Year Plan*, National Climate Program Office, National Oceanic and Atmospheric Administration, Washington, D.C., 101 pp.

North, G. R., and J. A. Coakley, Jr. (1979). Differences between seasonal and mean annual energy balance model calculations of climate and climate sensitivity, *J. Atmos. Sci. 36*, 1189.

Ohring, G. (1979). The effect of aerosols on the temperatures of a zonal average climate model, *Pageoph. 117*, 851.

Ohring, G., and P. Clapp (1980). The effect of changes in cloud amount on the net radiation at the top of the atmosphere, *J. Atmos. Sci. 37*, 447.

Parkinson, C. L., and W. W. Kellogg (1979). Arctic sea ice decay simulated for a CO_2-induced temperature rise, *Clim. Change 2*, 149.

Parkinson, C. L., and W. M. Washington (1979). A large-scale numerical model of sea ice, *J. Geophys. Res. 84*, 311.

Patterson, E. M. (1981). Optical properties of the crustal aerosol: relation to chemical and physical characteristics, *J. Geophys. Res. 86*, 3236.

Patterson, E. M., D. A. Gillette, and B. H. Stockton (1977). Complex index of refraction between 300 and 700 nm for Saharan aerosols, *J. Geophys. Res. 82*, 3153.

Pearman, G. I., ed. (1980). *Carbon Dioxide and Climate: Australian Research*, Proceedings of a symposium sponsored by the Australian Academy of Sciences, Canberra, Sept. 1980, 217 pp.

Peterson, G. M., T. Webb III, J. E. Kutzbach, T. van der Hammen, T. A. Wijmstra, and F. A. Street (1979). The continental record of environmental conditions at 18,000 yr BP: an initial evaluation, *Quat. Res. N.Y. 12*, 47.

Petukhov, V. K., Ye. M. Feygelson, and N. I. Manuylova (1975). The regulating role of clouds in the heat effects of anthropogenic aerosols and carbon dioxide, *Izv. Atmos. Oceanic Phys. 11*, 802.

Pfeffer, R. L., G. Buzyna, and R. Kung (1980). Relationships among eddy fluxes of heat, eddy temperature variances and basic-state temperature parameters in thermally driven rotating fluids., *J. Atmos. Sci. 37*, 2577.

Pittock, A. B. (1980). Toward a warm Earth scenario for Australia, in *Carbon Dioxide and Climate: Australian Research*, G. I. Pearman, ed., Australian Academy of Science, Canberra, pp. 197–209.

Plass, G. N. (1956a). The carbon dioxide theory of climatic change, *Tellus 8*, 140.

Plass, G. N. (1956b). Effect of carbon dioxide variations on climate, *Am. J. Phys. 24*, 376.

Pollack, J. B., O. B. Toon, C. Sagan, A. Summers, B. Baldwin, and W. Van Camp (1976). Volcanic explosions and climatic change: a theoretical assessment, *J. Geophys. Res. 81*, 1071.

Porch, W. M., and M. C. MacCracken (1982). Parametric study of the effects of Arctic soot on solar radiation, *Atmos. Environ.* (in press).

President's Science Advisory Committee (1965). Appendix Y4, *Restoring the Quality of Our Environment*, Report of the Environmental Pollution Panel, The White House, Washington, D.C., pp. 112-133.

Rahn, K. A., and R. J. McCaffrey (1980). On the origin and transport of the winter Arctic aerosol, in *Aerosols: Anthropogenic and Natural, Sources and Transport*, T. J. Knelp and P. J. Lioy, eds., *Ann. N.Y. Acad. Sci. 338*, 486-503.

Ramanathan, V. (1975). Greenhouse effect due to chlorofluorocarbons: climatic implications, *Science 190*, 50.

Ramanathan, V. (1980). Climatic effects of anthropogenic trace gases, in *Interactions of Energy and Climate*, W. Bach, J. Pankrath, and J. Williams, eds., D. Reidel, Boston, Massachusetts, pp. 269-280.

Ramanathan, V. (1981). The role of ocean-atmosphere interactions in the CO_2-climate problem, *J. Atmos. Sci. 38*, 918.

Ramanathan, V., and R. E. Dickinson (1979). The role of stratospheric ozone in the zonal and seasonal radiative energy balance of the Earth-troposphere system, *J. Atmos. Sci. 36*, 1084.

Ramanathan, V., M. S. Lian, and R. D. Cess (1979). Increased atmospheric CO_2: zonal and seasonal estimates of the effect on the radiation energy balance and surface temperature, *J. Geophys. Res. 84*, 4949.

Rasmussen, R. A., and M. A. K. Khali (1981). Increase in the concentration of atmospheric methane, *Atmos. Environ. 15*, 883.

Reck, R. A., and D. L. Fry (1978). The direct effects of chlorofluoromethanes on the atmospheric surface temperature, *Atmos. Environ. 12*, 2501.

Revelle, R., and H. E. Suess (1957). Carbon dioxide exchange between atmosphere and ocean and the question of an increase of atmospheric CO_2 during the past decades, *Tellus 9*, 18.

Roosen, R. G., R. J. Angione, and G. H. Klemcke (1973). Worldwide variations in atmospheric transmission: 1. Baseline results from Smithsonian observations, *Bull. Am. Meteorol. Soc. 54*, 307.

Rosen, J. M. (1971). The boiling point of stratospheric aerosols, *J. Appl. Meteorol. 10*, 1044.

Rowland, F. S., and M. J. Molina (1975). Chlorofluoromethanes in the environment, *Rev. Geophys. Space Phys. 13*, 1.

Ruddiman, W. F., and A. McIntyre (1979). Warmth of the subpolar north Atlantic Ocean during northern hemisphere ice-sheet growth, *Science 204*, 173.

SCEP (1970). *Man's Impact on the Global Environment*, Report of the Study of Critical Environmental Problems, MIT Press, Cambridge, Massachusetts.

Schlesinger, M. E. (1982). The climatic response to doubled CO_2 simulated by the OSU atmospheric GCM with a coupled swamp ocean, Climatic Research Institute, Oregon State U., Corvallis (in preparation).

Schneider, S. H. (1975). On the carbon dioxide-climate confusion, *J. Atmos. Sci. 32*, 2060.

Schneider, S. H., and S. L. Thompson (1981). Atmospheric CO_2 and climate: importance of the transient response, *J. Geophys. Res. 86*, 3135.

Schneider, S. H., W. M. Washington, and R. M. Chervin (1978). Cloudiness as a climatic feedback mechanism: effects on cloud amounts of prescribed global and regional surface temperature changes in the NCAR GCM, *J. Atmos. Sci. 35*, 2207.

References

Shaw, G. (1981). Column integrated aerosols in the Arctic and Antarctic, *J. Appl. Meteorol.* (submitted).
SMIC (1971). *Inadvertent Climate Modification*, Report of the Study of Man's Impact on Climate, MIT Press, Cambridge, Massachusetts.
Stumm, W., ed. (1977). *Global Chemical Cycles and Their Alterations by Man*, Proceedings of the Dahlem Workshop, Berlin, November 15-19, 1976, Abakon Verlagsgesellschaft, Berlin, German Federal Republic, 347 pp.
Thompson, S. L., and S. H. Schneider (1981). Carbon dioxide and climate: ice and ocean, *Nature 290*, 9.
Tyndall, J. (1863). On radiation through the Earth's atmosphere, *Philos. Mag. 4*, 200.
U.S. Committee for the Global Atmospheric Research Program (1975), *Understanding Climatic Change: A Program for Action*, National Academy of Sciences, Washington, D.C., 239 pp.
U.S. Department of Energy (1979). *Workshop on the Global Effects of Carbon Dioxide from Fossil Fuels*, Carbon Dioxide Effects Research and Assessment Program Rep. No. 001, CONF-770385, National Technical Information Service, Springfield, Virginia.
Vinnikov, K. Ya., and P. Ya. Groisman (1981). An empirical model of present-day climate changes, *Meteorol. Gidrol. 3*, 25-36.
Vinnikov, K. Ya., G. V. Gruza, V. F. Zakharov, A. A. Kirillov, N. P. Kovyneva, and E. Ya. Ran'kova (1980). Contemporary variations of the northern hemisphere climate, *Meteorol. Gidrol. 6*, 5.
Wang, W.-C., and P. H. Stone (1980). Effect of ice-albedo feedback on global sensitivity in a one-dimensional radiative-convective climate model, *J. Atmos. Sci. 37*, 545.
Wang, W. C., Y. L. Yung, A. A. Lacis, T. Mo, and J. E. Hansen (1976). Greenhouse effects due to man-made perturbations of trace gases, *Science 194*, 685.
Wang, W.-C., W. B. Rossow, M.-S. Yao, and M. Wolfson (1981). Climate sensitivity of a one-dimensional radiative-convective model with cloud feedback, *J. Atmos. Sci. 38*, 1167.
Warren, S. G., and S. H. Schneider (1979). Seasonal simulation as a test for uncertainties in the parameterizations of a Budyko-Sellers zonal climate model, *J. Atmos. Sci. 36*, 1377.
Weiss, R. F. (1981). The temporal and spatial distribution of tropospheric nitrous oxide, *J. Geophys. Res. 86*, 7185-7195.
Wetherald, R. T., and S. Manabe (1975). The effect of changing the solar constant on the climate of general circulation model, *J. Atmos. Sci. 32*, 2044.
Wetherald, R. T., and S. Manabe (1981). Influence of seasonal variation upon the sensitivity of a model climate, *J. Geophys. Res. 86*, 1194.
Wigley, T. M. L., and P. D. Jones (1981). Detecting CO_2-induced climate change, *Nature 292*, 205.
Wigley, T. M. L., P. D. Jones, and P. M. Kelly (1980). Scenario for a warm, high-CO_2 world, *Nature 283*, 17.
Williams, J., ed. (1978). *Carbon Dioxide, Climate and Society*, IIASA Proceedings Series: Environment (International Institute for Applied Systems Analysis, Laxenburg, Austria), Pergamon Press, Oxford, 332 pp.
Williams, J. (1980). Anomalies in temperature and rainfall during warm Arctic seasons as a guide to the formulation of climate scenarios, *Clim. Change 2*, 249.
World Meteorological Organization (1979a). *Proceedings of the World Climate Conference*, WMO Rep. No. 537, World Meteorological Organization Secretariat, Geneva, Switzerland, 791 pp.
World Meteorological Organization (1979b). *Report of the First Session of the CAS Working Group on Atmospheric Carbon Dioxide*, WMO Project on Research and Monitoring of

Atmospheric CO_2, Rep. No. 2, Commission for Atmospheric Sciences, World Meteorological Organization, Geneva, Switzerland, 49 pp.

World Meteorological Organization (1981). *Joint WMO/ICSU/UNEP Meeting of Experts on the Assessment of the Role of CO_2 on Climate Variations and Their Impact*, Joint Planning Staff, World Meteorological Organization, Geneva, Switzerland, 35 pp.